Imago Mundi

V

Paolo Pellizzari

One Billion Indians

CONTINENTS

Art Director
Fayçal Zaouali

Editorial Coordinator
Paola Gallerani

Editing
A. H. Maines

5 Continents Editions
Via Canonica 13
20154 Milan (Italy)
Tel. +39 02 33603276
Fax +39 02 312377
info@5continentseditions.com

Paolo Pellizzari is represented by the VU Agency (Paris)
for France and the rest of the world; by Grazia Neri
Agency (Milan) for Italy.
E-mail: paolo@pellizzari.net

Color Separation
Galasele, Milan

Printed September 2003
by Leva Arti Grafiche, Sesto San Giovanni (Milan)
for 5 Continents Editions, Milan
Printed in Italy

Table of Contents

Acknowledgments

I would like to thank Nathalie and Guy Trouveroy, Sumant Rai Dewan
and his team, Devika Daulat-Singh and her team, Alka Pande and her
team, Patricia Uberoi, T. Narayan, Vinod Mehta, Barbara Piovan, and
Raman Naahar, all of whom made a contribution at various stages of
this book.

I would also like to point out that despite numerous trips to India and
considerable travel within the country, at no point was I ever robbed or
attacked; nor did I encounter violence of any kind. I met many friendly,
helpful people—some of whom have now become good friends.
Considering the conditions in which some of these people live, their
comportment provides an example to aspire to for our own countries.

"Reality surpasses the resources of my imagination and never ceases to fill me with astonishment and admiration."

Michel Tournier

"The crowd is his element, as the air is that of birds and water of fishes. His passion and his profession are to become one flesh with the crowd. For the perfect flaneur, for the passionate spectator, it is an immense joy to set up house in the heart of the multitude, amid the ebb and flow of movement, in the midst of the fugitive and the infinite. To be away from home and yet to feel oneself everywhere at home; to see the world, to be at the centre of the world, and yet to remain hidden from the world—impartial natures which the tongue can but clumsily define. The spectator is a prince who everywhere rejoices in his incognito... Or we might liken him to a mirror as vast as the crowd itself; or to a kaleidoscope gifted with consciousness, responding to each one of its movements and reproducing the multiplicity of life and the flickering grace of all the elements of life."

Charles Baudelaire

"The Flaneur". In *The Painter of Modern Life. Modern Life and Other essays*. Trans. by Jonahtan Mayne. New York: da Capo Press 1964, pp. 9-12 (ed. or: *Le peintre de la vie moderne, Figaro,* 26th and 29th November, 3rd December 1863).

Note From the Author

Contents

This book is essentially a compilation of ordinary life scenes, taken in streets and public locations around India. It is neither the best nor the worst of what there is to see, but lies somewhere in between. It is not meant as a travelogue or a personal story. This book is a document showing hundreds of details of today's India, shot in many different regions over a period of four years, starting in 1999.

The format of the photographs is panoramic, giving each picture the grand feeling of an opera stage. Every person, every detail is there to bewilder the viewer with strong yet confusing feelings, similar to those I experienced while taking the picture.

About the title

It is obviously provocative and somewhat pretentious to call a book of photographs *One Billion Indians*. No one can claim to cover the full diversity of a country this size. Many things are missing; entire provinces, different religions or ethnic groups, social representations… Nevertheless, I stubbornly held on to this title despite the misgivings of many friends whose opinions I usually respect.

There are many reasons for this.

The first is that *One Billion Indians* is the most important key to understand the country. It is the factor that determines its physical aspect, its architecture, its logistics, its public transportation, and therefore shapes the impression one has when observing it. This information lies at the core of politics and religious beliefs, and is magnified by the country's rapid urban growth.

The second reason is more personal. The title relates to my panoramic eye, to the idea of showing one billion details, one billion attitudes, one billion feelings - harmony within complexity.

So, while there is a risk that some Indians will not recognize themselves in this book, my intention is not to offend them or their country, but to celebrate it—a country where beauty is found in all shapes, where hospitality is deeply imbedded in people's nature.

Paolo Pellizzari

India's Population at a Glance*

*Source: *Provisional Population Totals: India. Census of India 2001*, Series 1, India.

The World's most Populous Countries

Country	Reference date	Population (in millions)
China	01/02/2000	1,277.6
India	01/03/2001	1,027.0
U.S.A.	April, 2000	281.4
Indonesia	01/07/2000	212.1
Brazil	01/07/2000	170.1
Pakistan	01/07/2000	156.5
Russian Fed.	01/07/2000	146.9
Bangladesh	01/07/2000	129.2

Population Density, India: 1941–2001

Census year	Density (per sq. km)
1941	103
1951	117
1961	142
1971	177[1]
1981	216[2]
1991	267[2]
2001	324[2]

Notes:
1. Kashmir has been excluded as comparable figures of area and population are not available for that State.
2. The density has been worked out on comparable data.

India. Population Projection

Period	1996–2001	2011–2016
Projected Population (in millions)	1012.4 (2001)[1]	1263.5 (2016)[1]

Note:
1. Figures in the parentheses indicate the end year for which the corresponding projections have been made.

Source: *Population Projections for India and States: 1996-2016.* Registrar General, New Delhi, 1996.

Population Growth 1991–2001

Males	531,277,078
Females	495,738,169
Total	1,027,015,247

Absolute growth: 180,627,359 (21,34%)

Females per 1,000 males: 933

Patricia Uberoi

The other half-billion?
The complex politics of "representing" India

I saw Paolo's exhibition, "One Billion Indians", in circumstances rather different from the context of the present book. While this book only presents Paolo's panoramic photographic vignettes of India's complex variety of peoples and scenes, the photo-exhibition that I saw in New Delhi in February / March 2003 partnered Paolo's images with somewhat comparable photos from the contemporary archives of *Outlook* magazine, an Indian news magazine well-known for the excellent quality of its visual materials. The juxtaposition sought to address a certain incongruence that Paolo had experienced in public reactions to his photographs when he had exhibited in Brussels. While *European* viewers had mostly appreciated the color, congestion, chaos and untidiness captured in Paolo's panoramic views of everyday Indian life, many *Indian* viewers were obviously left feeling uncomfortable by the same images. A "rag-picker's perspective" is how one offended viewer put it.

Now, Indians living abroad are known to be extremely sensitive regarding their national image—something to do with the politics of their immigrant status on the one hand, and nostalgia for a remembered homeland on the other. And on the whole they prefer their culture to be represented abroad by the historical, the classical, the spiritual and the exquisite, or at least through the "folk"—but not through the "everyday" or, worse still, through *kitsch*.

But what of Indians "at home"? Do they see and represent India differently from the foreign photographer, and if so, what are the "politics" of this difference? Or do Indian photographers see themselves as others do; and if so, how is one to interpret this congruence? Or is it that the medium determines the message, as Marshall McLuhan suggested long ago? Of course, such questions are not specific to photography, but pertain to other arts as well. And they are also central issues for debate in the social science discipline to which I myself belong—Anthropology—which is defined as the study of "other" peoples. Indeed, anthropologists long believed that an outsider could see things more objectively than a native; a presumption that has been increasingly contested as anthropologists confront the unattractive record of their discipline's objectification of non-European peoples under the guise of scientific inquiry.

The Delhi exhibition could not really answer the questions it posed. For one thing, there is bound to be a difference between the *personal* vision of an individual photographer, and the *collective* vision of a half-dozen news photographers whose individual styles are moderated by editorial intervention. And there is obviously a difference of *genre* between the picaresque image captured by the wandering traveler—the *flaneur*—and the newsworthy visual addition to a news story. One could see this clearly in the photo captions (the former narrating a personal itinerary, sharing the moment of the image's capture; the latter simply labeling the scene), and generic difference is also embedded in the photographic techniques used. Paolo's "panoramic" technique produces an interesting distortion of vision, meant to emphasize otherwise ineffable characteristics of the scene as *personally* experienced, while the news-photographer is meant to create the impression of unmediated realism, however contrived his photo might actually be.

While it could not provide answers, the juxtaposition of foreign and local photographers in the Delhi exhibition provoked one to consider whether and in what ways Paolo's vision of India might be essentially that of an *outsider*—his work ultimately rendering exotic, objectifying, perhaps even eroticizing, the country and its people. Let us consider briefly some aspects of this question.

To begin with, take the exhibition title, "One Billion Indians", on which Paolo himself has been both apologetic and defensive. On the one hand, except perhaps in a census year, Indians do not usually perceive themselves as a huge round number of people. On the other hand, the "one billion" image taps into an invidious, century-old stereotype which construes Asia's teeming numbers as profoundly threatening to the life-styles and security of the sparsely populated countries of the North: ominous when these others are poor, backward and diseased and, if anything, even more so when they are economically prosperous.

A trifle ingenuously, perhaps, Paolo ignores such pervasive, negative stereotypes, explaining that he uses the title, "One Billion Indians", simply to emphasize, descriptively, the congestion and crowdedness of India and its infinite variety of peoples and scenes. Clearly, there is tension here, but interestingly it is tension that replicates the contradiction at the very heart of post-colonial India's nation-building project (antedating the West's belated discovery of the political virtues of multiculturalism): the simultaneous valorization of the principle of national unity along with the seemingly contradictory endorsement of cultural "diversity."

A second aspect of Paolo's outsider's perspective is his focus on the "everyday"—neither the exquisite nor the manifestly ugly, but something in-between: the beauty, surprise, irony and pathos of the most ordinary of views. Here we have another sort of tension. By definition, the everyday is unremarkable, and it surely needs an outsider's eye to appreciate its facets. At the same time, what is everyday for the Indian is a *foreign* everyday for the European viewer, which may be more unfamiliar and exotic in its own way than the well-known scenes of international tourist attractions, or the Indian tourist industry's stereotypical iconic portraits of tribal beauties and weather-beaten peasant faces. After all, the intention *is* to catch the viewer's eye.

Moreover, insofar as there is a politics of *genre*, one could also say that Paolo's choice of the picaresque mode (rather than, say, the "photo-essay"), and his panoramic photographic technique (rather than "flat" pictures) also work as distancing devices, rendering the object of vision exotic, even when that object is merely everyday.

Personally, I dispute the contention that focusing on the everyday necessarily amounts to a "rag-picker's perspective." All the same, one must also allow that this focus may ultimately lend beauty and exoticism to realities which, in themselves, are unattractively grim. It is a thin line to skirt. The brilliant photograph of cavernous rows of LIG (Low Income Group) houses that Paolo used as his exhibition icon is a case in point: *exotic* (imagine houses used as billboards!), and *aesthetic* (radiant colors against a cloud-filled, sunny sky; a strikingly beautiful composition). One can almost forget that *people*, hundreds and thousands of them, live out their lives cheek-by-jowl in the sunless interiors of this housing estate, set in some unkempt urban wilderness. Dwarfed beside the towering advertisements for products they themselves can ill afford, their billboard-dwellings are just an exotic, panoramic flash of color seen from the adjacent highway. True, as Paolo says, the panoramic photography technique draws the viewer viscerally along with the photographer *into* the scene; but not to join the people—these tiny dots on a cityscape—who live there. Rather, the viewer is invited to inscribe his own product advertisement on one of the blank, stark white walls, marked only with a contact phone number. Suddenly, here, the *flaneur* loses his old-world detachment and becomes, without warning, a powerful photographic critic of the dehumanized developmental agenda of a post-liberalized Indian state.

While foreign and local photographers in the Delhi exhibition objectified their subjects rather differently, in at least one respect they were strikingly similar. They presented India primarily as a male domain, conspicuously neglecting the other half a billion—*female*—people; excluding the female spectator from the inclusiveness of their panoramic visions. Paolo shows us the musty library of the Kolkata High Court, packed with (male) lawyers; the Technicolor interior of a barber's shop; the Kafka-esque scene of a policeman presiding over shelves of dust-laden files in a Mughal-period basement; the reception line of clamorous white-clad men awaiting the arrival of foreign tourists; men and motorcycles against a tangle of wires and fuse boxes; a stream of villagers pushing earnestly across a level crossing; Sikh temple functionaries counting treasury taxes: *male* protagonists and *male* spaces all. And where women are present, they are often seen only at a great distance (as in the view of the Shillong vegetable market). They lack individuality; or they are of India's "other" races; or they occupy peripheral positions in the photo-frame; or their gaze is elsewhere. A little girl asleep on her father's cot in a courtyard full of sleeping men and boys attracts attention precisely *because* she is visibly out of place. The face of the mother of a handicapped boy is half-cropped out of the frame, avoiding the pathos of their relationship. And a scene of Indian families lounging on the lawns around India Gate, Delhi, is tritely unconvincing, having neither the aesthetic attraction nor the emotional charge of so many of Paolo's other photographs.

While regretting the absence of India's other half billion, one may also note the more positive side of this absence: At least Paolo (and the *Outlook* photographers as well) managed to avoid—and perhaps took special pains to avoid—Indian tourism's neo-Orientalist photo-promotion of Indian feminine beauty: color, adornment, winsomeness, perhaps even bare tribal breasts! One acknowledges this self-restraint, even while wondering whether a feminine sensibility behind the camera would (or would not) have seen India's "one billion" rather more inclusively. For the truth is that one cannot say that Paolo is an outsider whose camera has failed to represent the real, true and complete India; merely that he is *just a man* who has met with the reverse glass partition between India's two worlds—male and female.

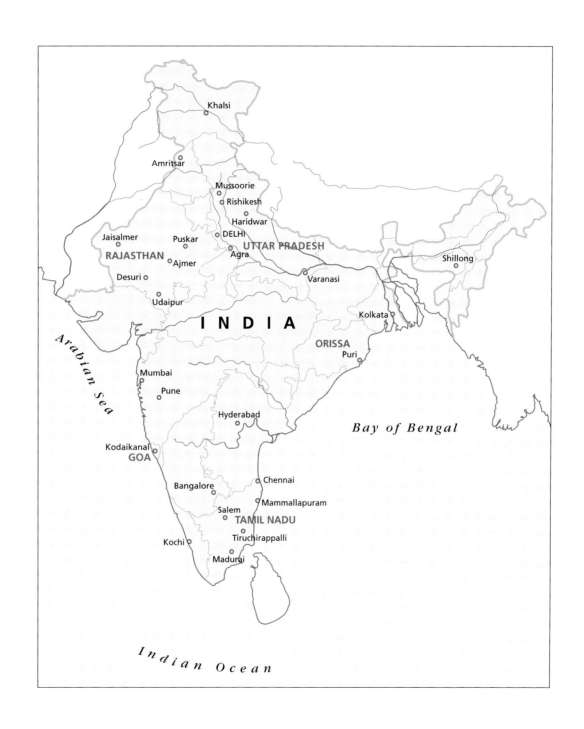

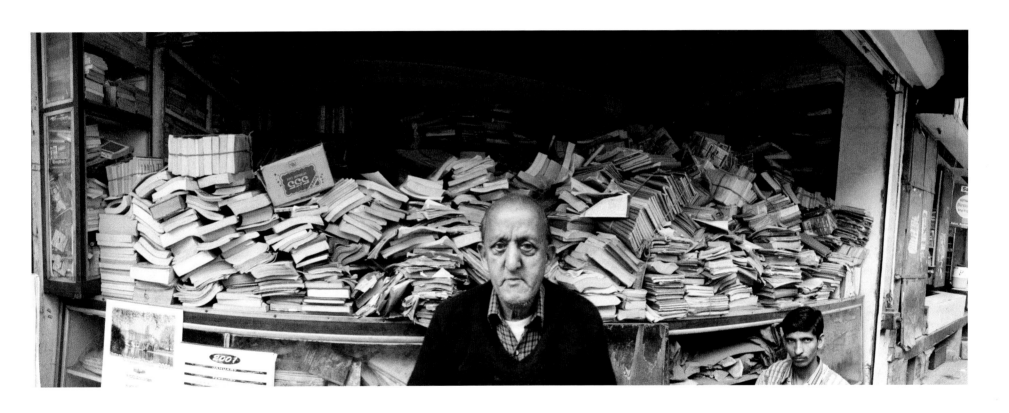

Delhi, Bookshop Owner and Assistant, 2001

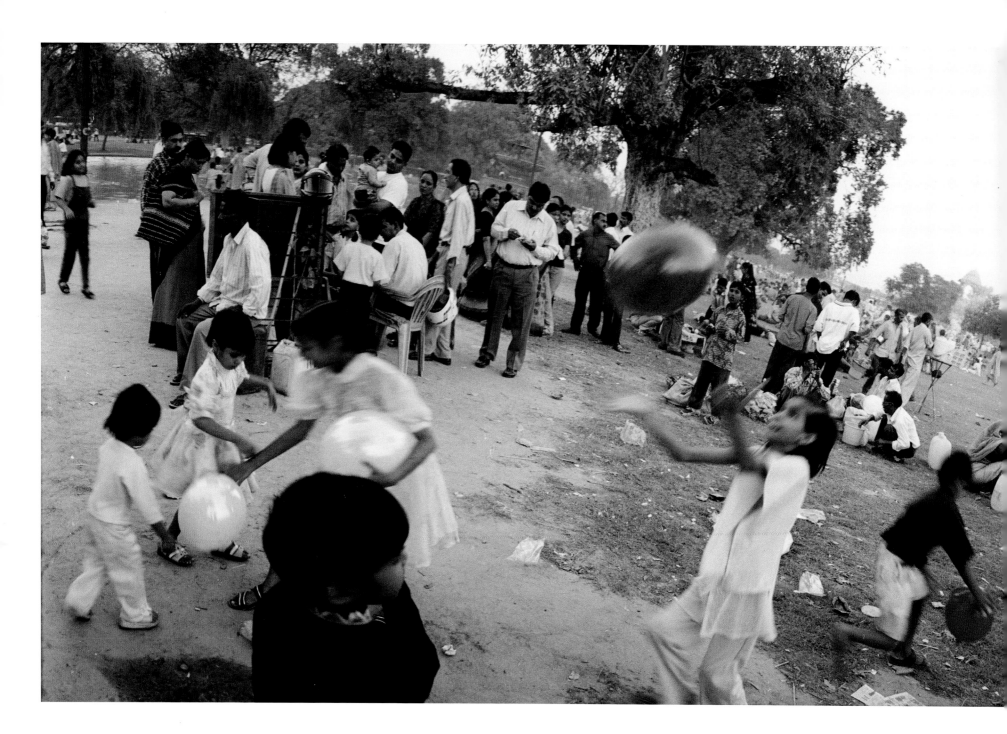

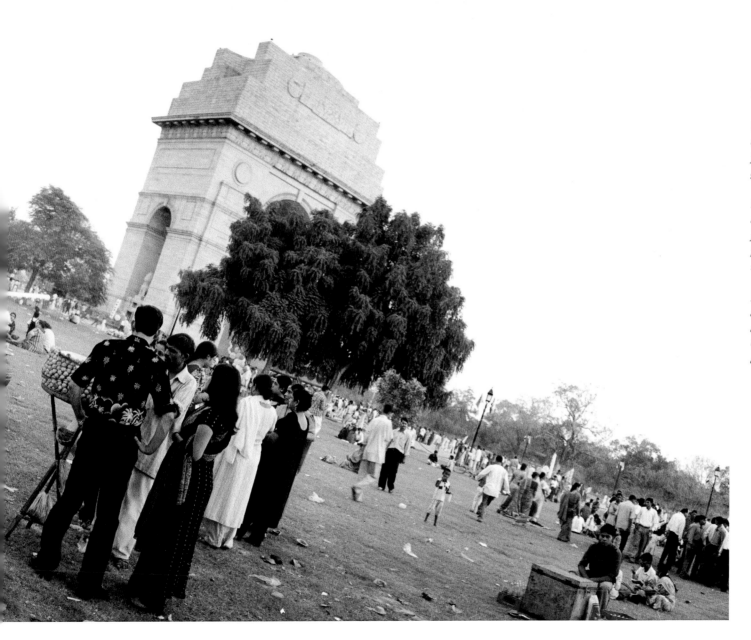

Delhi, India Gate on Sunday, 2002

*On a Sunday afternoon, the park in front
of India Gate becomes a large playground where
families express the sheer joy of being there: simple
games, sociability and a blessing of the week.*

*Le dimanche après-midi, le parc devant la Porte
de l'Inde devient un vaste terrain de jeux où les
familles montrent leur plaisir de se retrouver :
jeux simples, rencontres sociales, un des bons
moments de la semaine.*

*La domenica pomeriggio, il parco di fronte
all'India Gate diventa un enorme campo da gioco
dove le famiglie esprimono la gioia di trovarsi lì.
Giochi semplici, cordialità, festosa conclusione
della settimana.*

Delhi, India vs. Pakistan, 2003

Through the glass window of a TV shop a group of people watch the event of the season: The 2003 Cricket World Cup Match between India and Pakistan.

À travers la vitrine d'une boutique de téléviseurs, un groupe de spectateurs regarde l'événement de la saison: le match de la Coupe du monde de cricket 2003 entre l'Inde et le Pakistan.

Attraverso la vetrina di un negozio di elettrodomestici un gruppo di persone guarda in televisione l'evento della stagione: l'incontro fra India e Pakistan per la coppa del mondo di cricket del 2003.

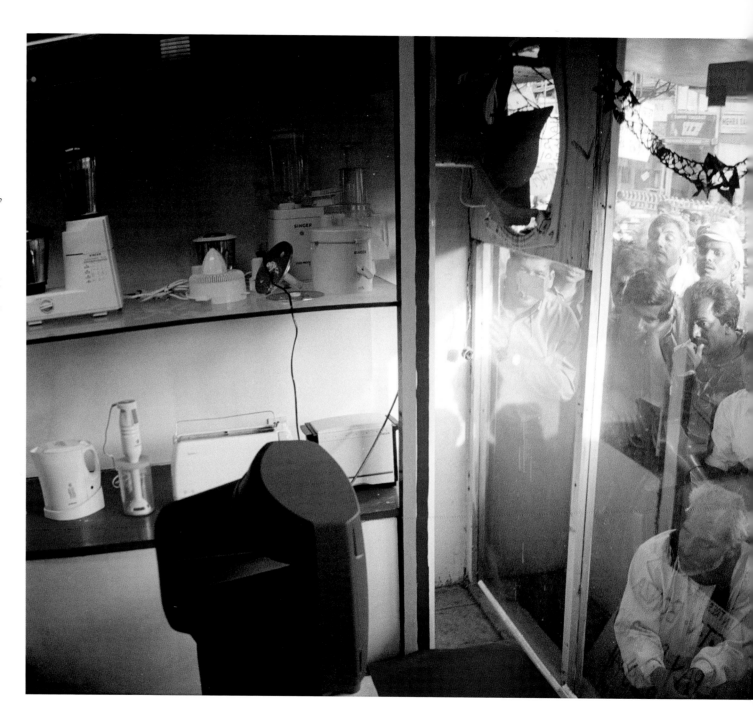

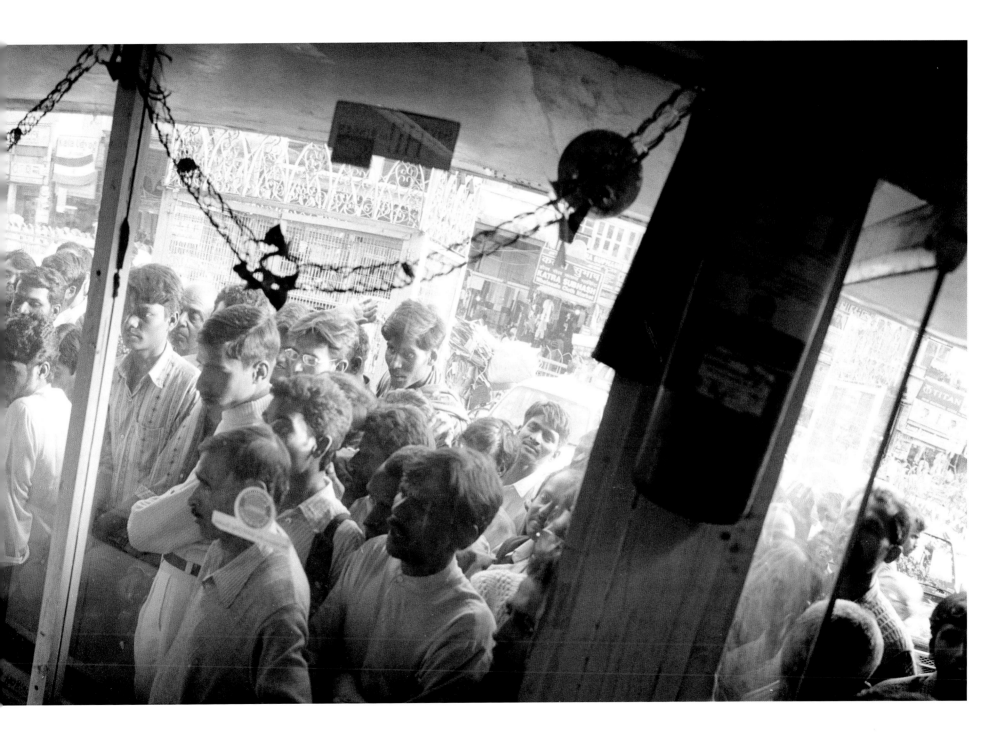

Delhi, Muslim Area, 2002

*After the Gujarat riots between Muslims and
Hindus, posters popped up on walls all over the
country. The tension could be felt even in
faraway Delhi, prompting one to wonder just
how fragile India really is.*

*Après les émeutes de Gudjarat entre musulmans
et hindous, des affiches furent placardées partout
dans tout le pays. La tension pouvait se sentir
même dans le lointain Delhi, ce qui fait réfléchir
sur la fragilité de l'Inde actuelle.*

*Dopo i tumulti di Gujarat fra musulmani e indù,
in tutto il paese, persino nella lontana Delhi,
sono apparsi manifesti sui muri: la tensione era
percepibile e fa riflettere sulla fragilità dell'India
contemporanea.*

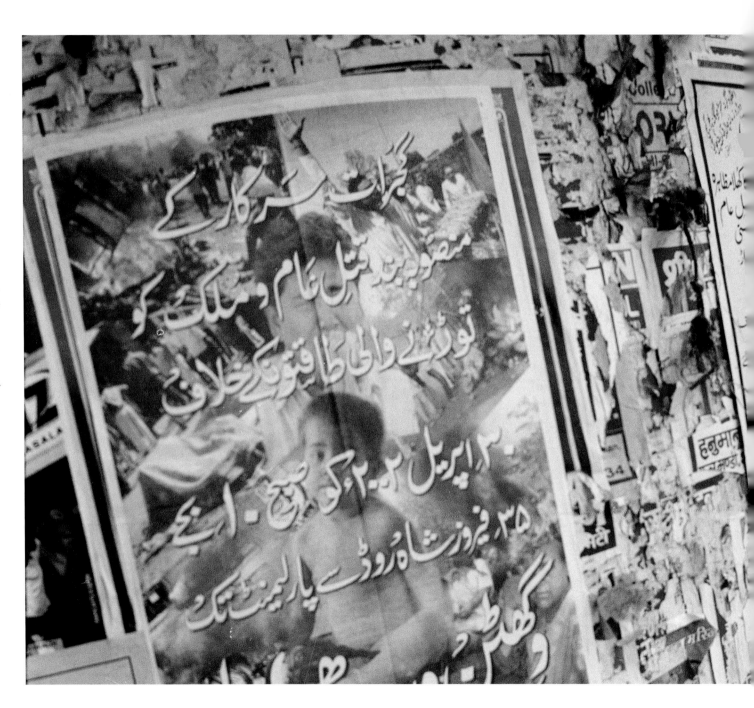

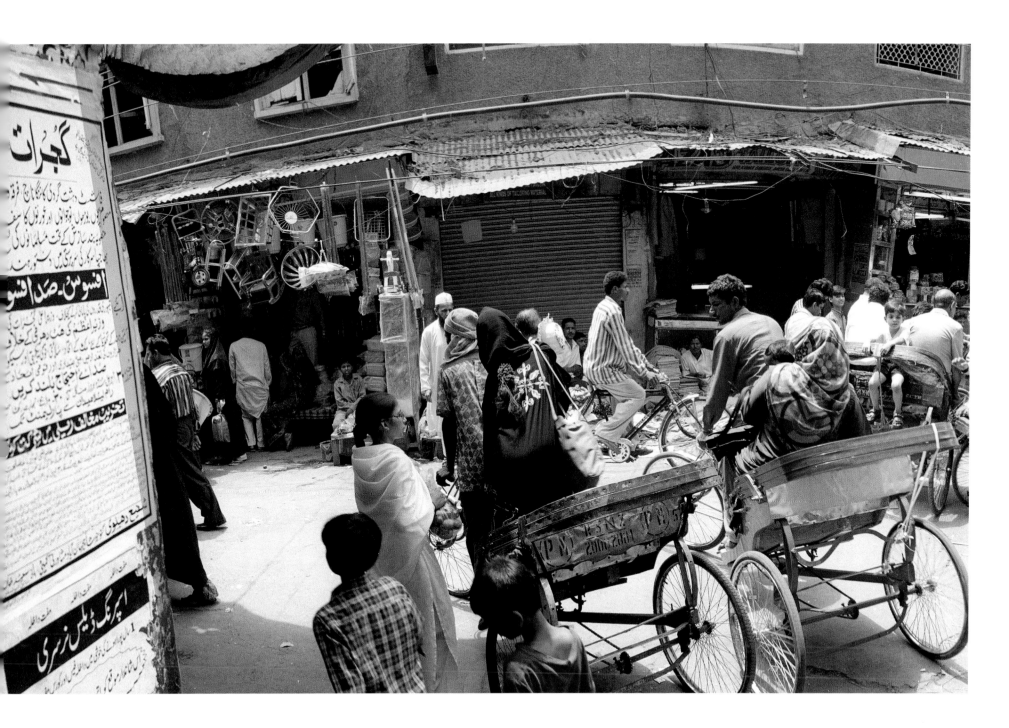

Delhi, Archives, 2002

In the Mogul cellar of what was once Frase's House, a guard shows us the Railway Administration archives: managed chaos amidst layers of history.

Dans les caves datant de l'époque moghole de ce qui fut jadis Frase's House, un garde nous montre les archives de l'administration des chemins de fer. Un chaos géré, des strates de l'histoire.

Nella cantina moghul di quella che un tempo era Frase's House, una guardia ci mostra gli archivi dell'amministrazione ferroviaria: caos sotto controllo, stratificazioni di storia.

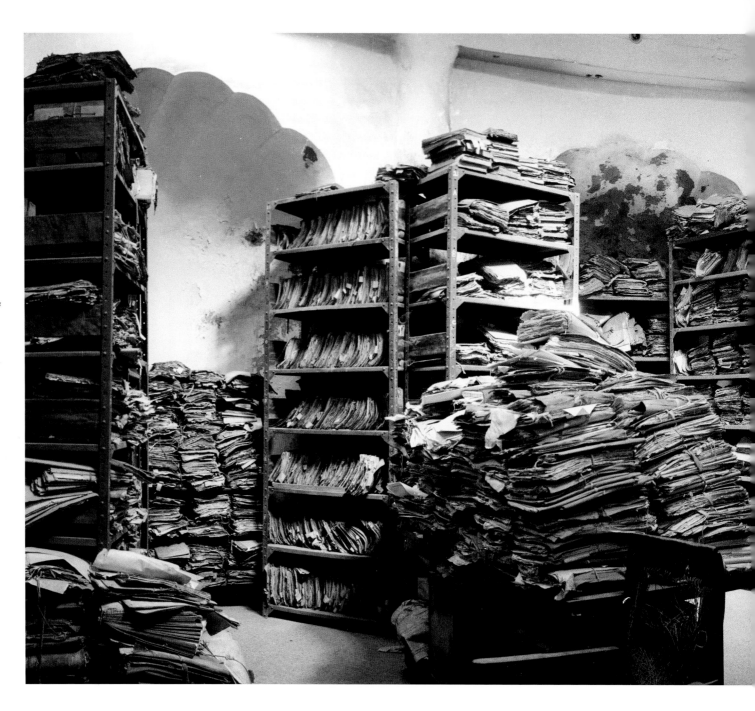

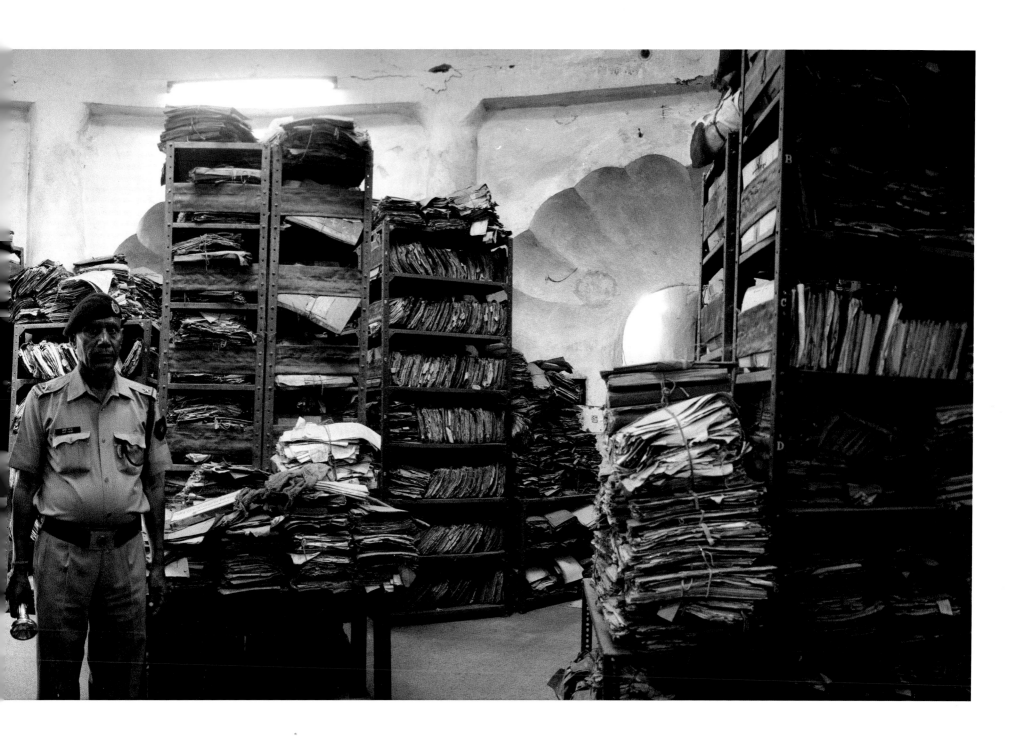

Delhi, Heroes, 2001

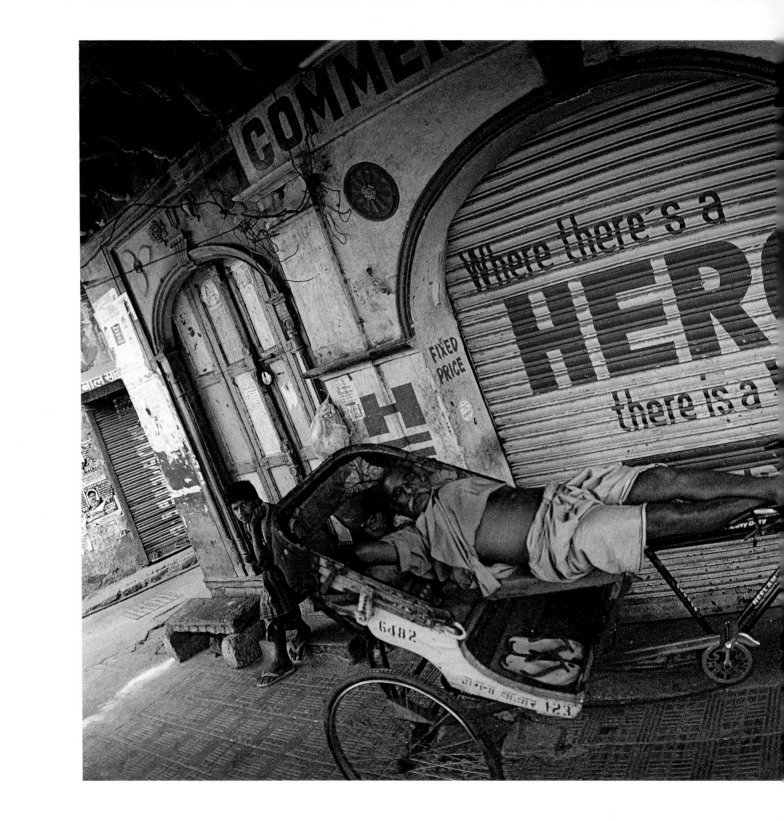

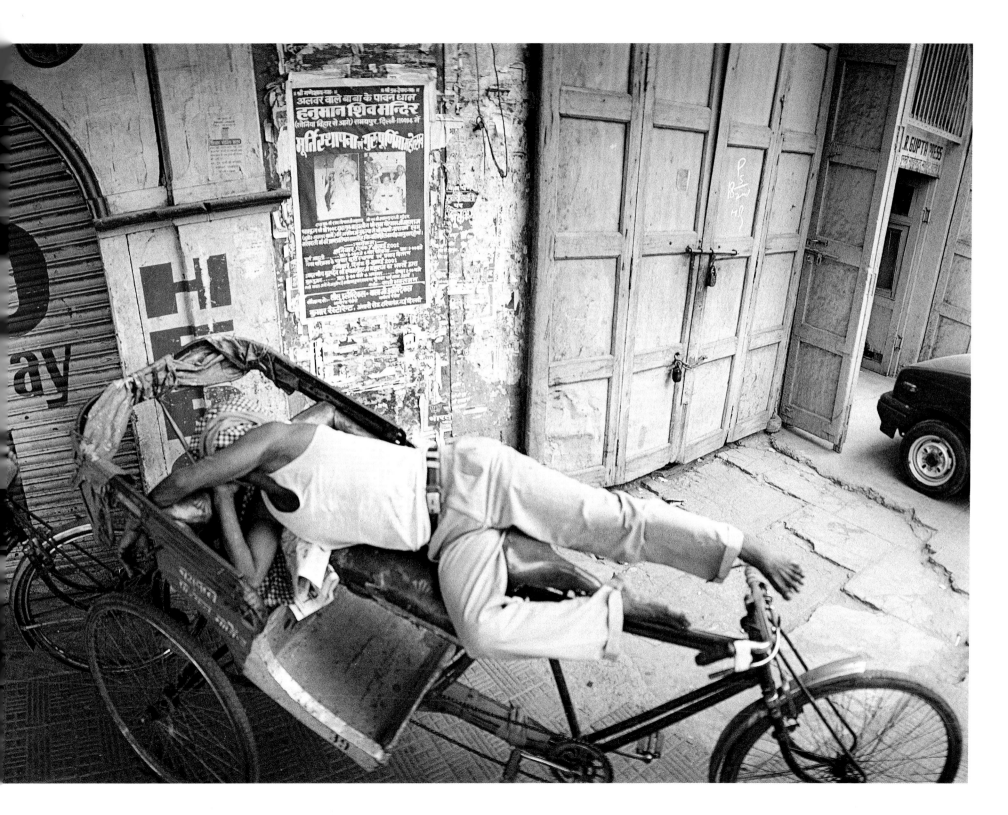

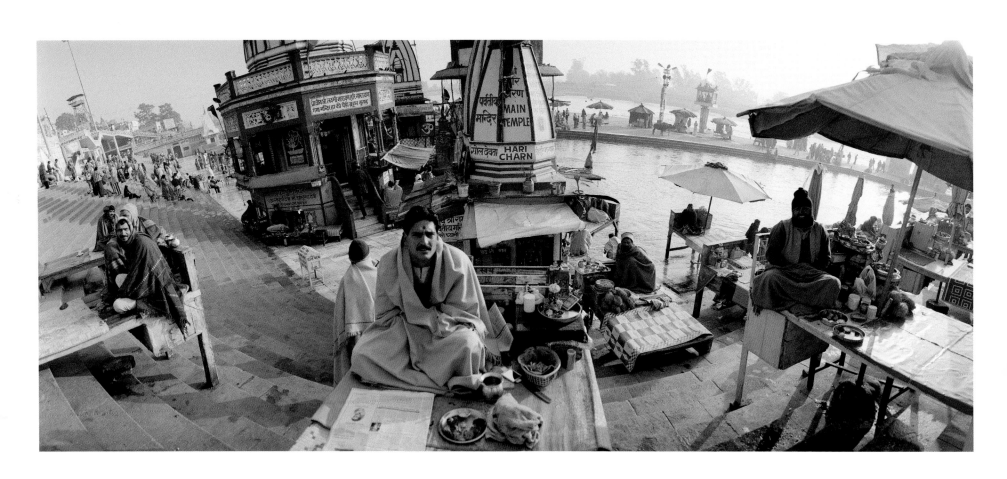

Haridwar Gates, Offering Stands, 2001

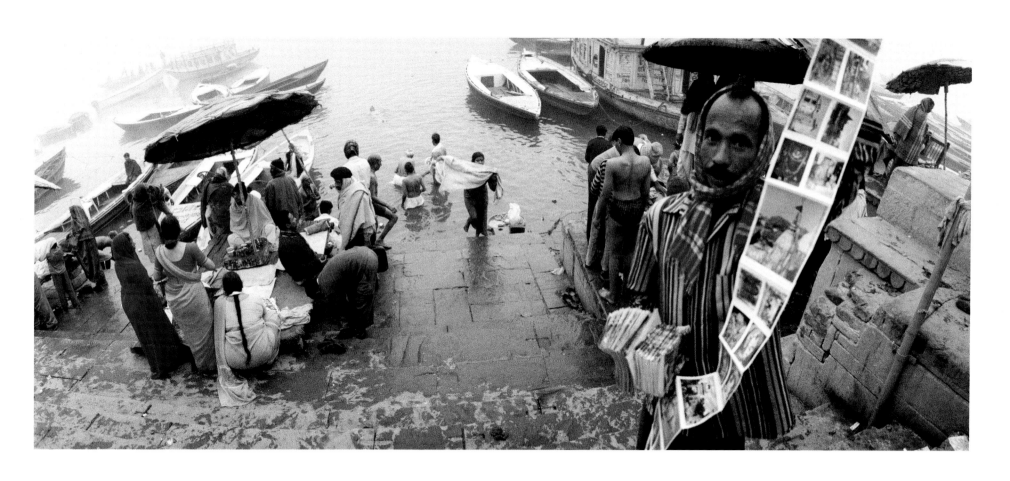

Varanasi, Gange and Postcards, 2001

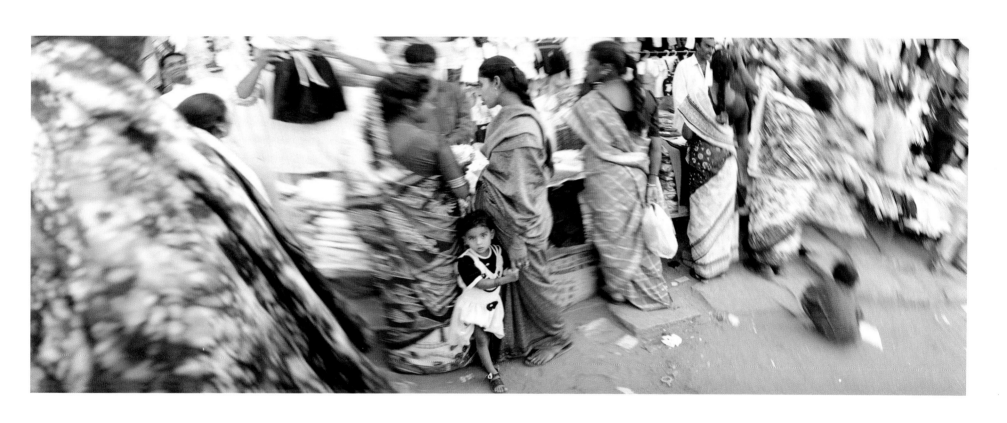

Hyderabad, Street Shopping, 2002

Hyderabad, Make-up, 2002

*In a local theater, actors put on make-up
for the comedy they are about to perform before
a large audience. Tickets cost between
20 and 50 cents.*

*Dans un théâtre de la ville, un groupe
d'acteurs se maquillent pour la comédie qu'ils
vont jouer; le public sera nombreux. La place
coûte entre 20 et 50 centimes.*

*In un teatro della città un gruppo di attori
si trucca in attesa di recitare una commedia.
Il pubblico sarà numeroso: i posti costano
fra i 20 e i 50 centesimi.*

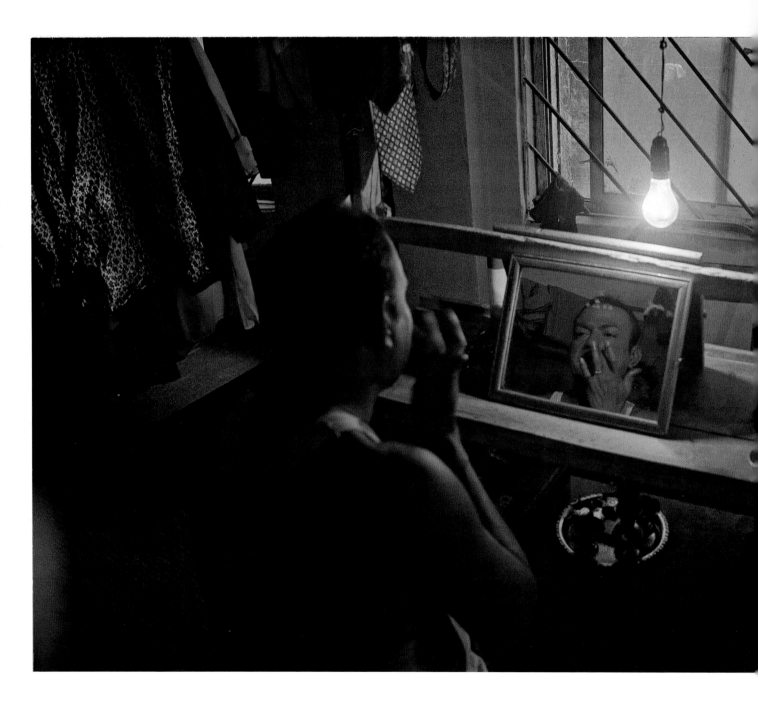

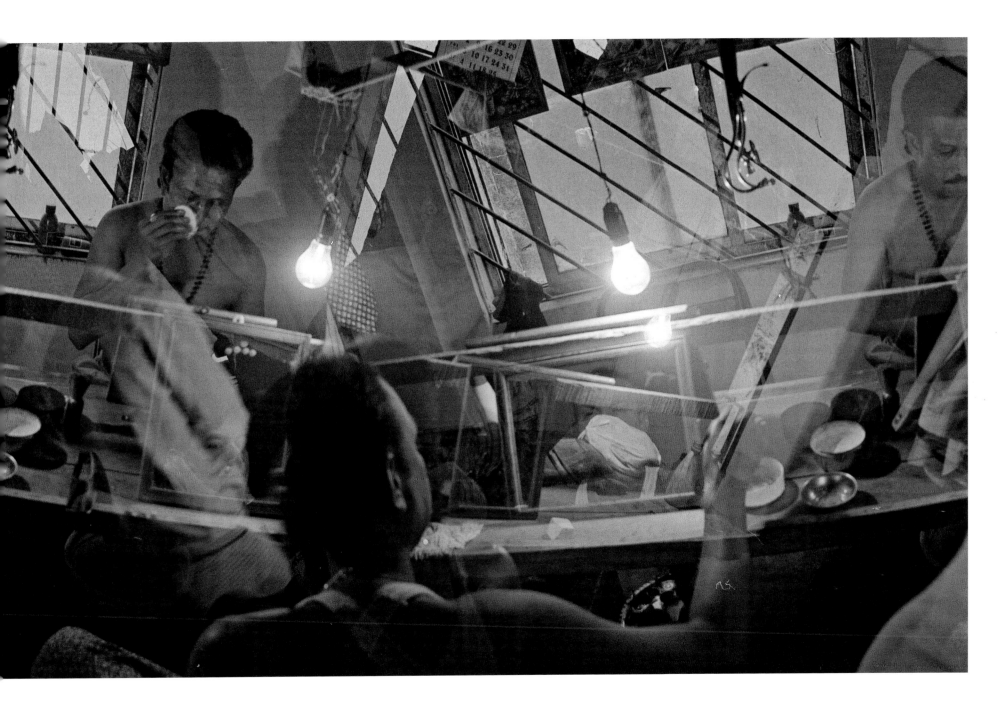

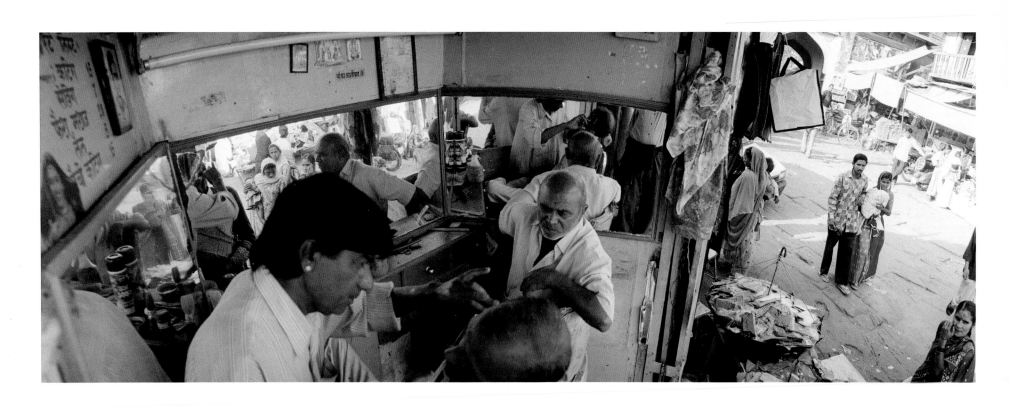

Jaisalmer, Barbershop, 2003

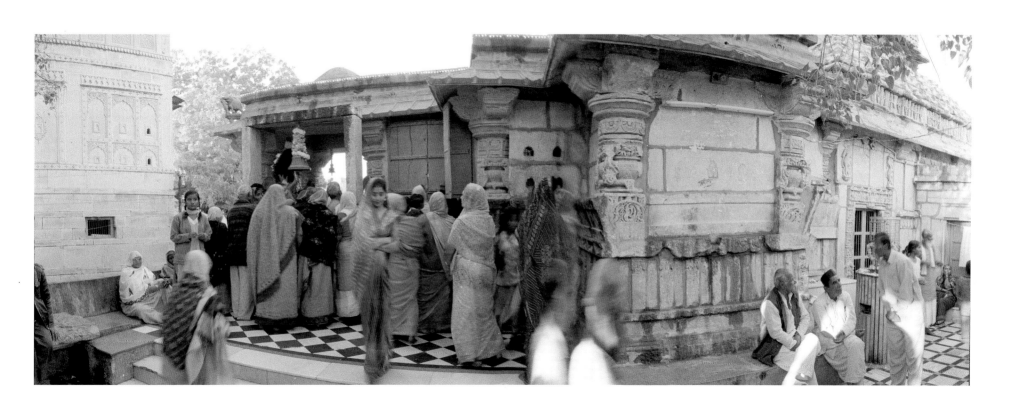

Jaisalmer, Princess at the Temple, 2003

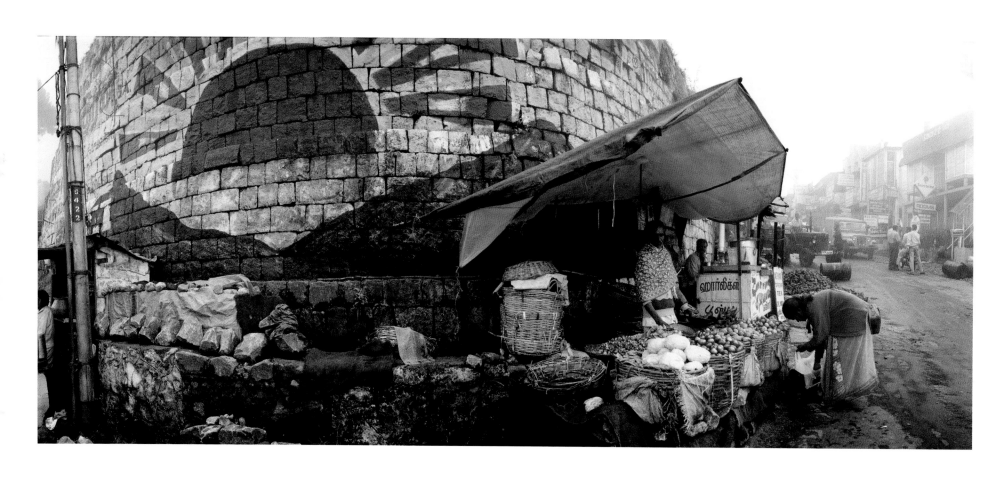

Kodaikanal, Misty Day, 2000

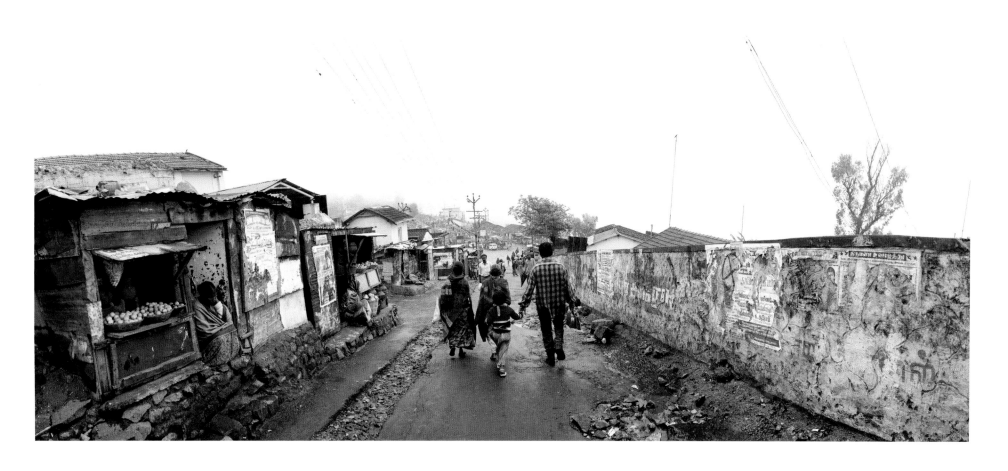

Kodaikanal, Path to Downtown, 2000
Kolkata, Transport of Tin Boxes, 2002 ▷

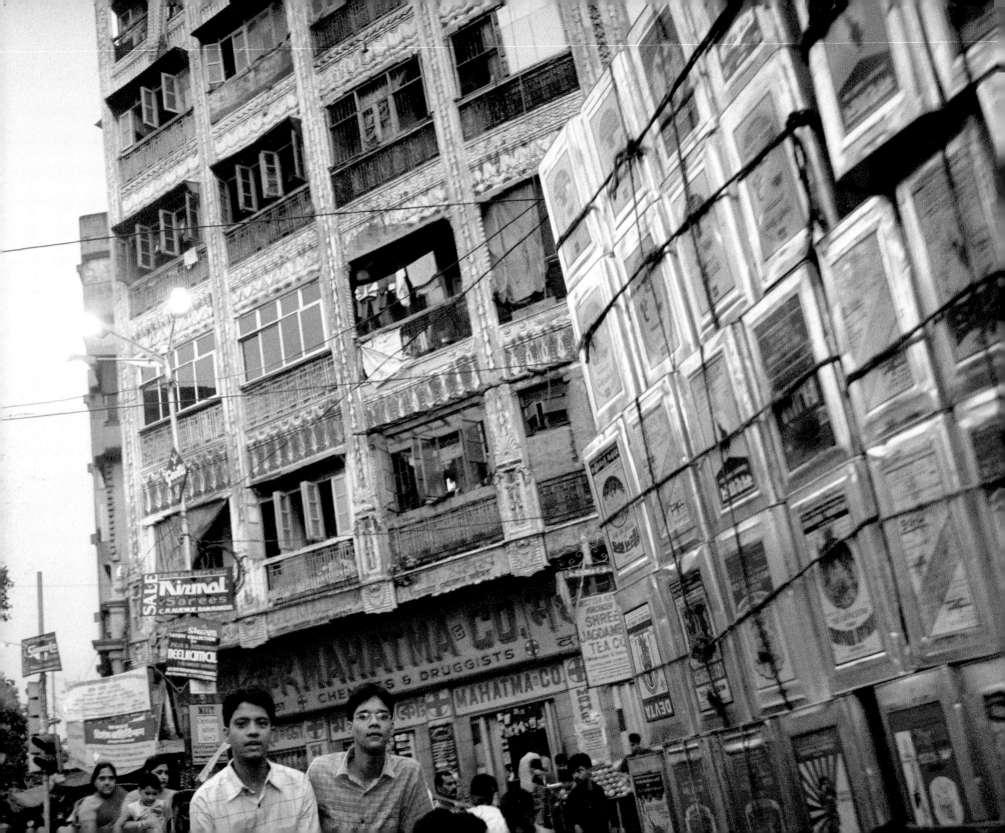

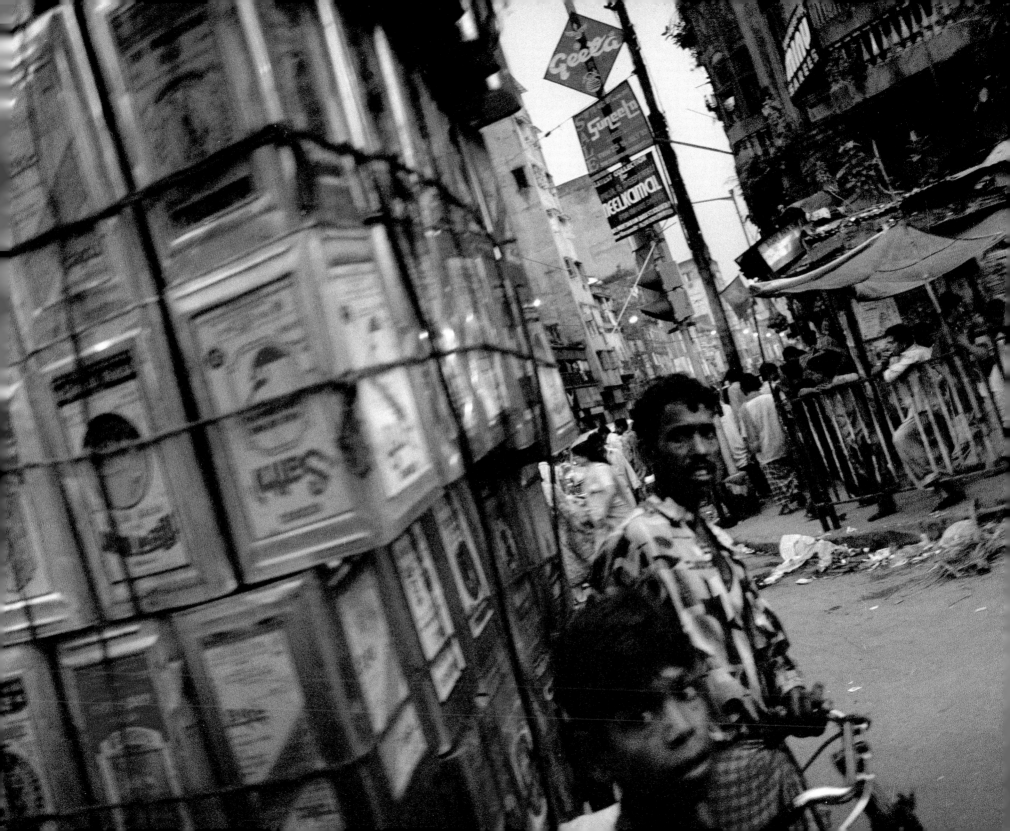

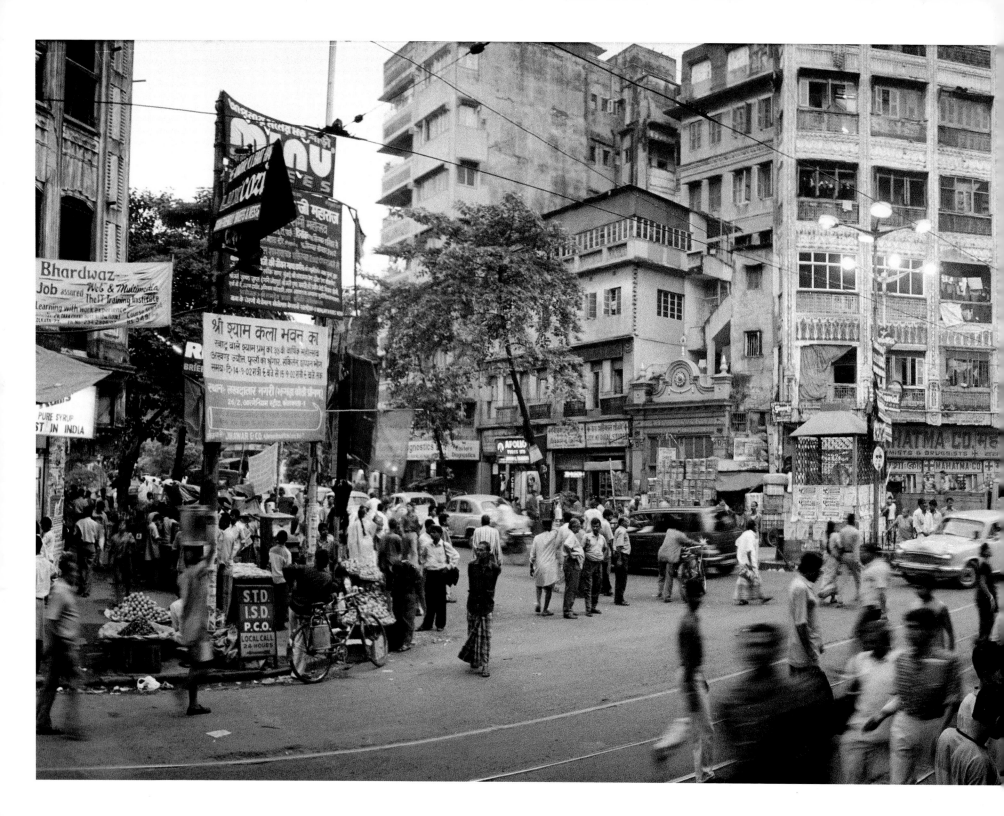

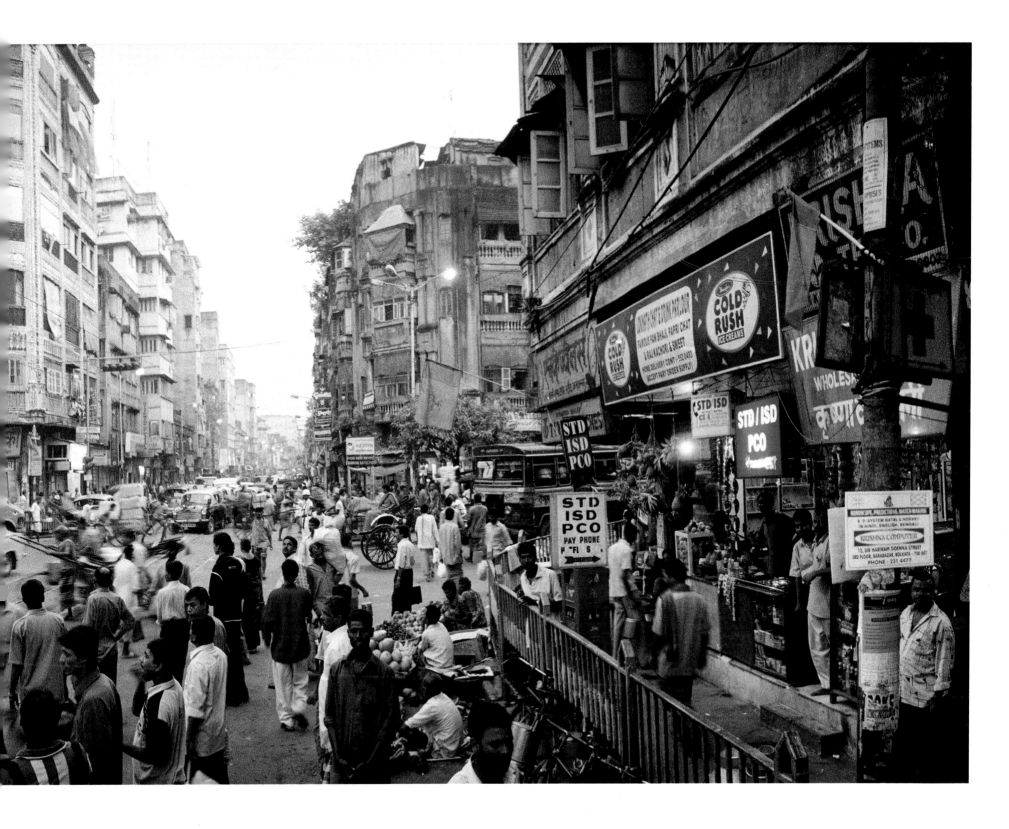

Kolkata, Coffee House, 2002

*Along the stairs at the entrance of this
extraordinary coffee house in the heart of Kolkata
University, posters line the walls like pop art.*

*Le long des escaliers de l'entrée de cet
extraordinaire café au cœur de l'université de
Kolkata, des affiches recouvrent le mur en une
fresque pop art.*

*Manifesti sulle scale del caffè come fossero
pop art. È l'ingresso di questo straordinario
caffè nel cuore dell'università di Kolkata.*

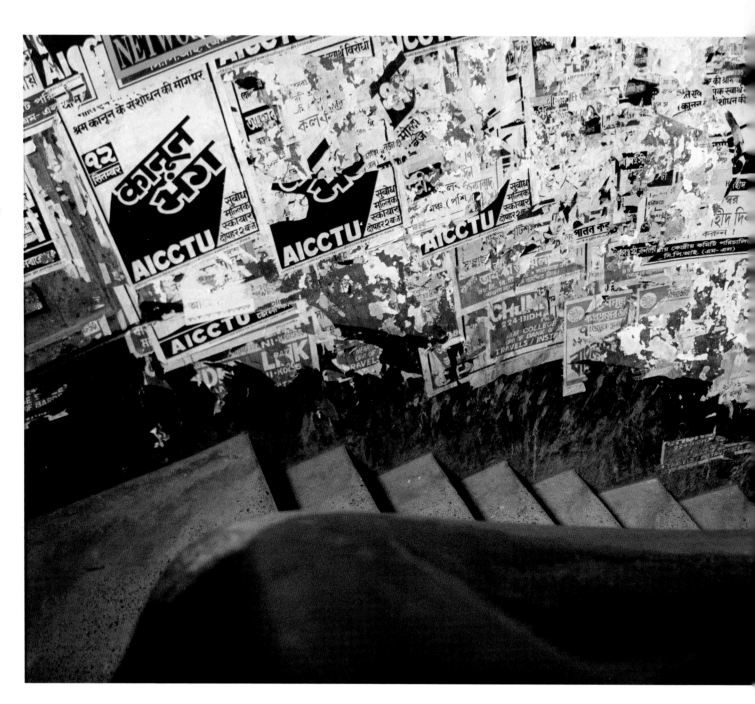

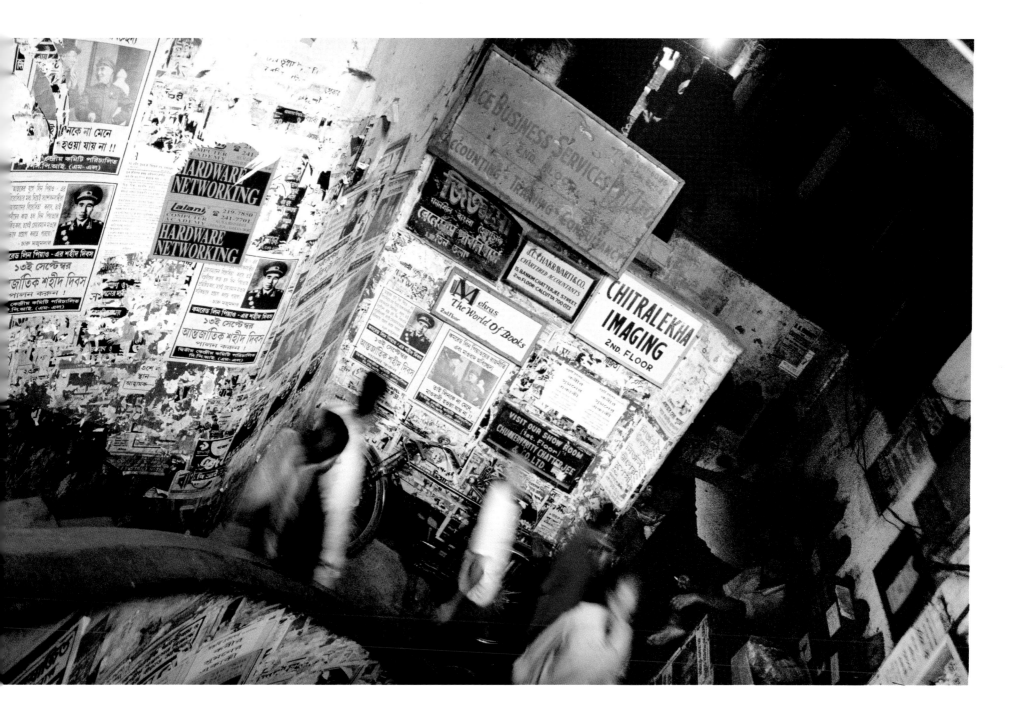

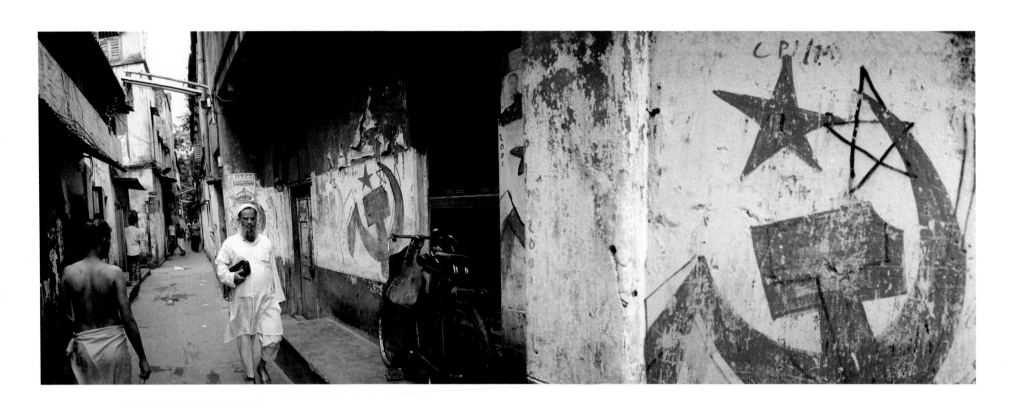

Kolkata, Communist Majority, 2002

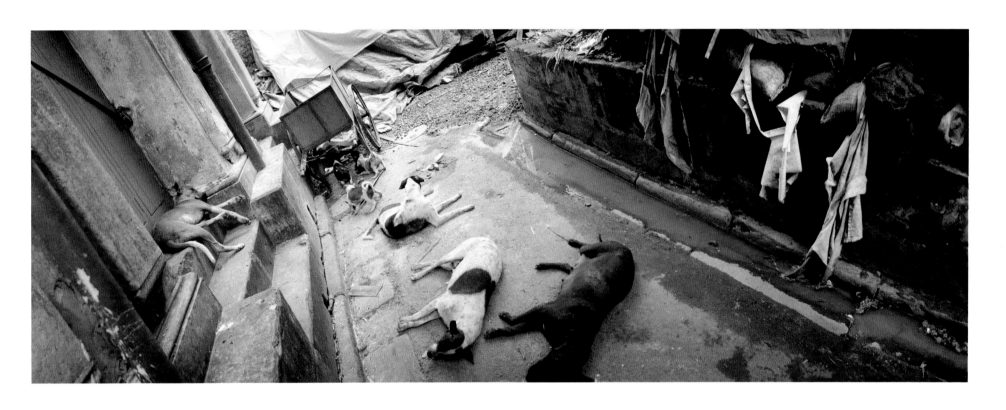

Kolkata, Dogs and Pigments, 2002
Kolkata, Afternoon Nap, 2002 ▷

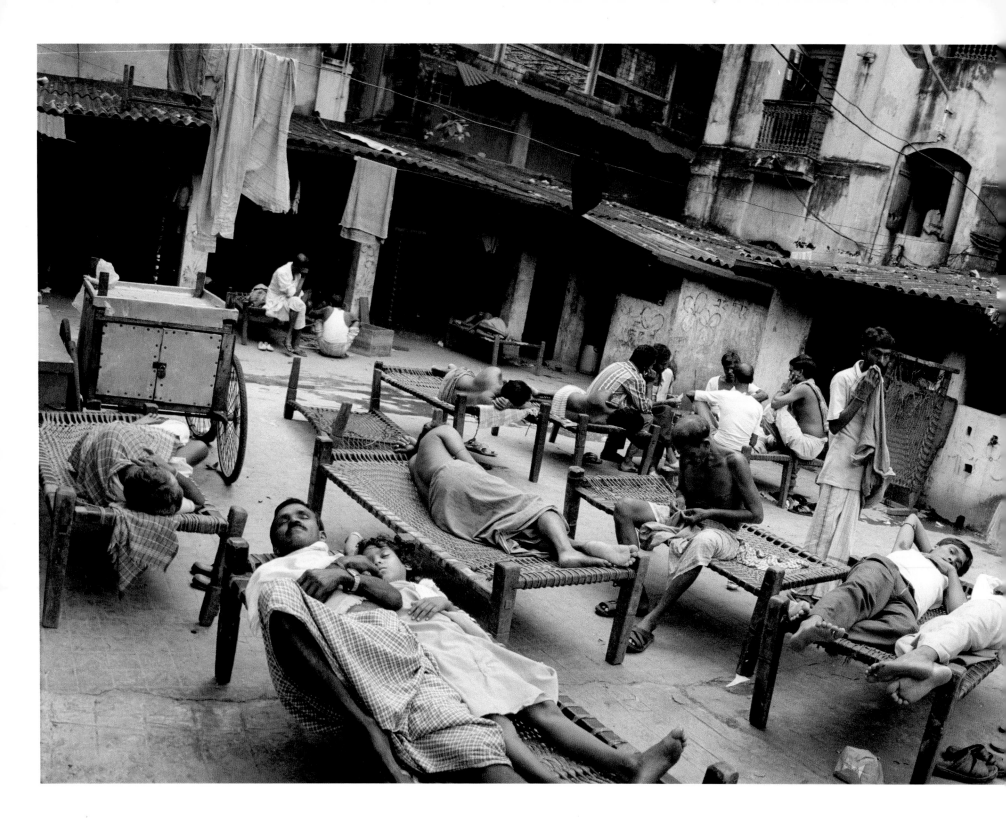

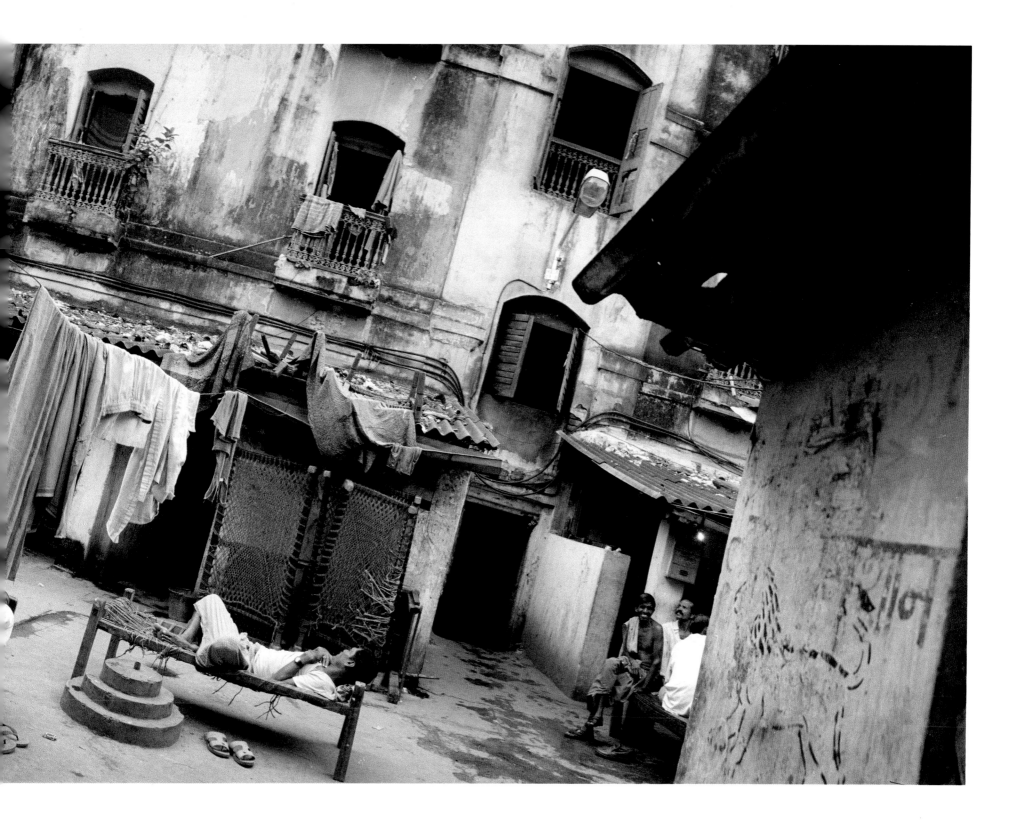

Kolkata, Cattle, 2002

Arriving early in the morning from out of town, hundreds of cattle cross a traffic-free city on their way to the slaughterhouses.

Très tôt le matin, des centaines de bêtes venues de la campagne traversent la ville encore vide de circulation pour se rendre aux abattoirs.

Al mattino presto, centinaia di ovini, provenienti dalla campagna, attraversano la città ancora senza traffico per andare al macello.

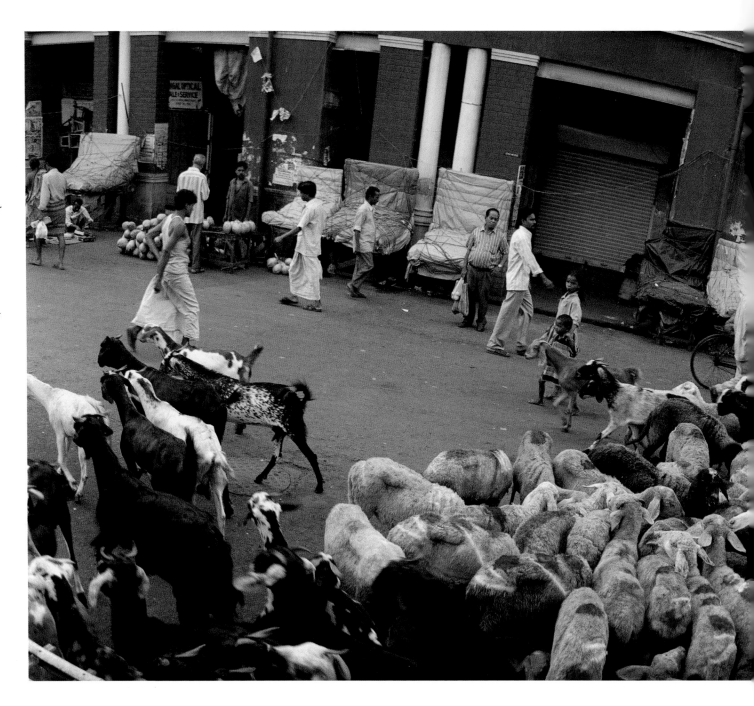

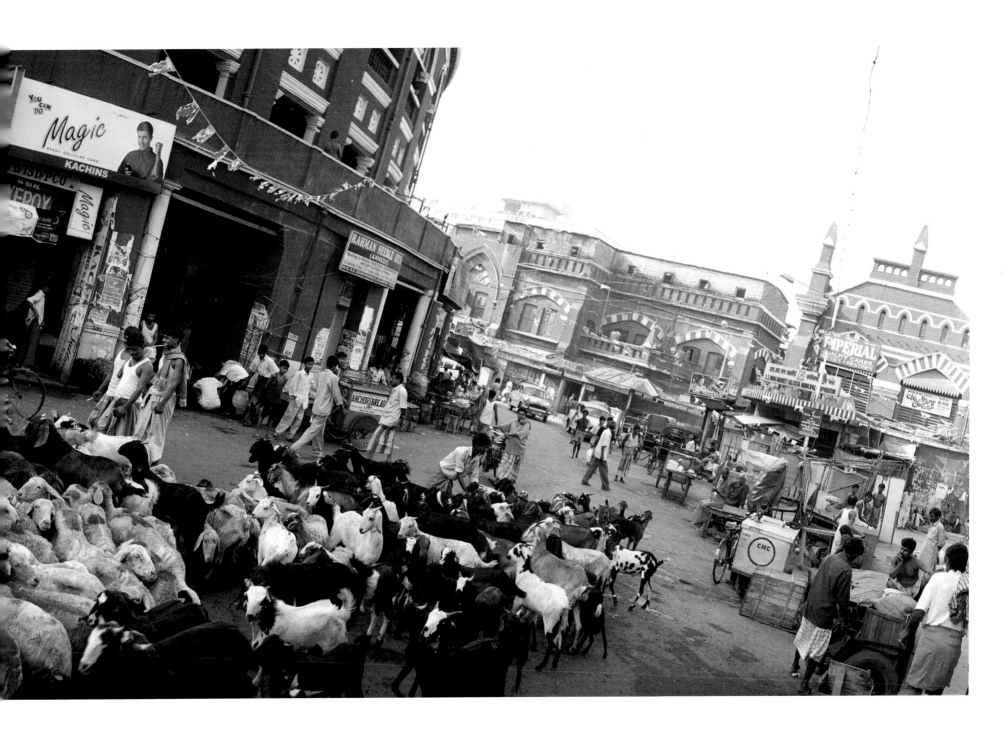

Kolkata, Counting Donations, 2001

On the first floor of a Sikh temple, the community is tallying donations collected during the last month. Every Sunday, these donations help feed a large number of people.

Au premier étage d'un temple sikh, la communauté compte les donations collectées au cours du mois précédent. Chaque dimanche, elles servent à nourrir un grand nombre de gens.

Al primo piano di un tempio sikh la comunità sta contando le donazioni ricevute nel corso dell'ultimo mese. Tali donazioni aiutano a sfamare ogni domenica moltissime persone.

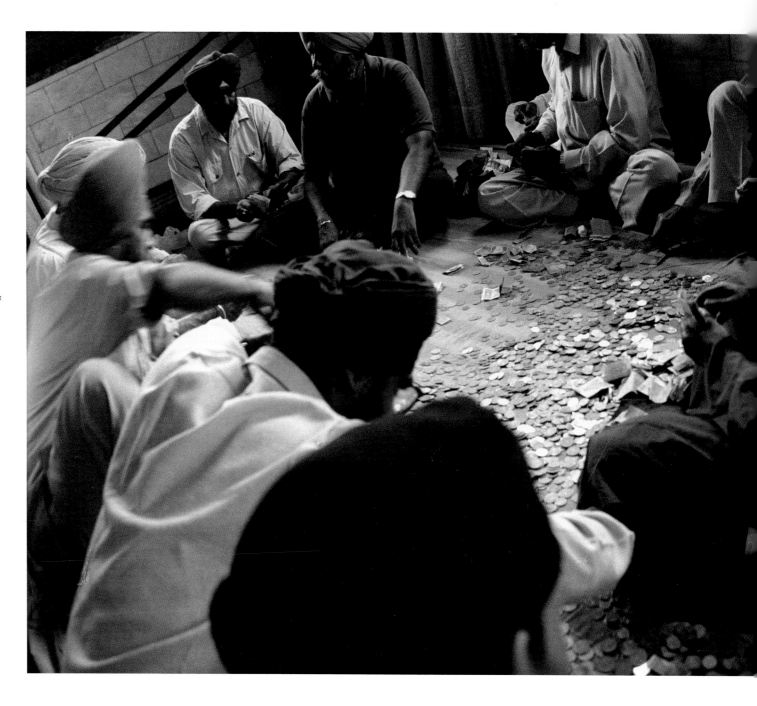

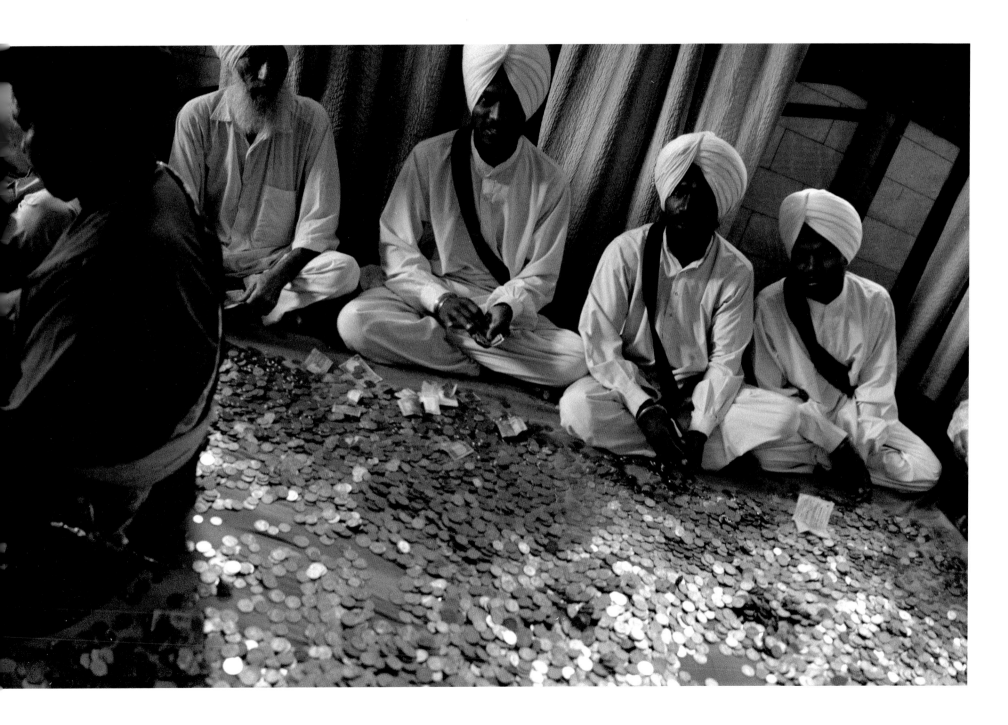

Kolkata, High Court Library ▷▷

I spent a long time with these attorneys,
enjoying a spirited conversation about India
and the best sites to visit. Then I took
this picture at a very low speed, capturing this
no man's land of knowledge where tradition and
civility have replaced conflict and arguments.

J'ai passé beaucoup de temps avec ces avocats
qui parlent avec esprit et intelligence de l'Inde et
des lieux à visiter. Puis j'ai pris à vitesse très
lente cette image de ce no man's land de la
connaissance, où la tradition et la civilité
remplacent les conflits et les disputes.

Ho trascorso parecchio tempo con questi
avvocati, che parlano con umorismo e intelligenza
dell'India e dei posti da vedere. Poi ho scattato
questa fotografia con un tempo molto lungo
e ho catturato questa no man's land della
conoscenza, là dove tradizione e civiltà prendono
il posto di liti e conflitti.

Kolkata, Train, 2002 ▷▷

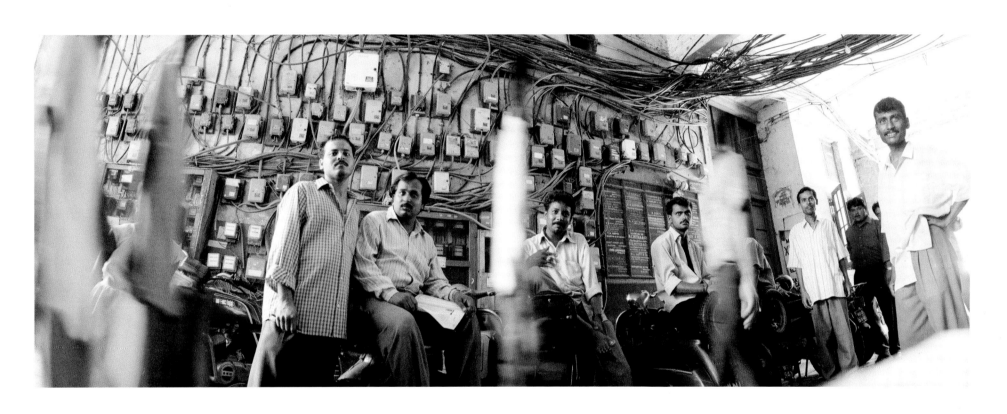

Kolkata, Electric Switchboard, 2002

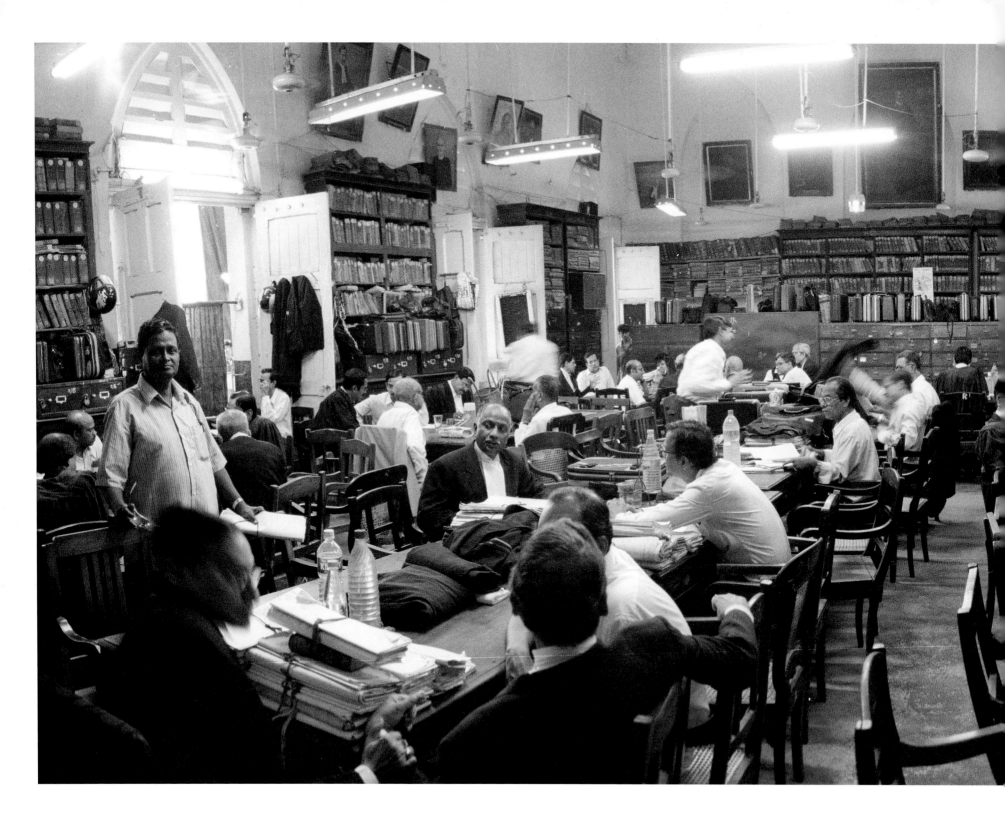

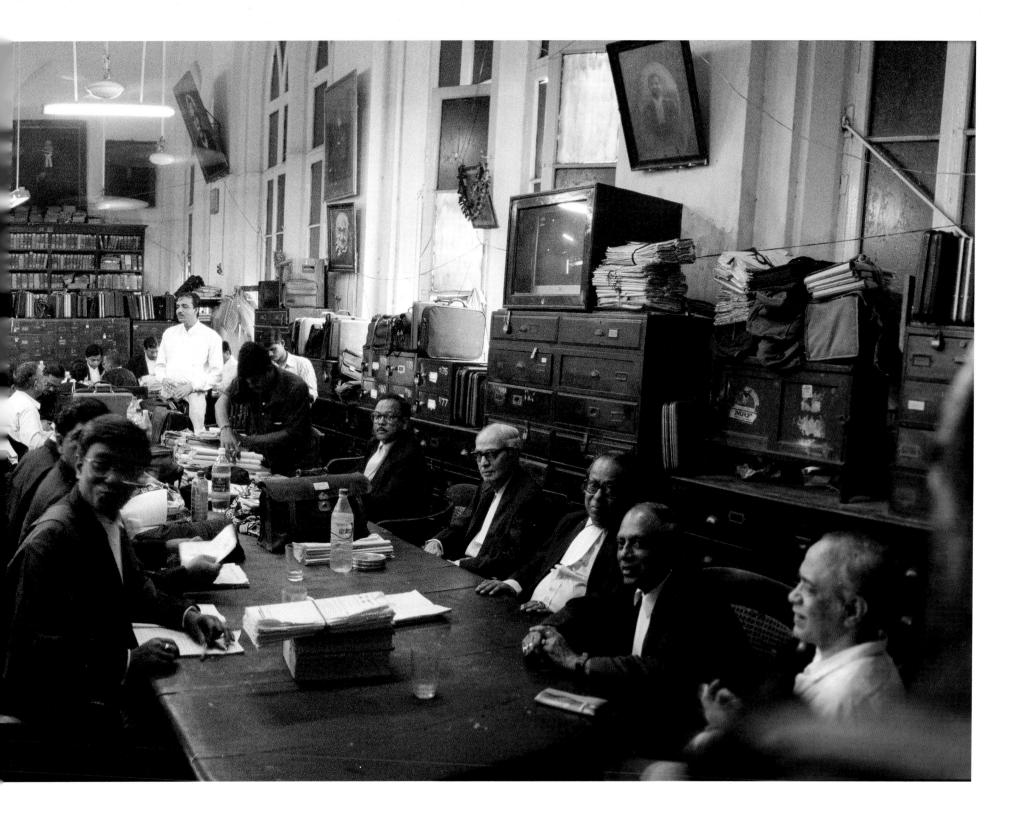

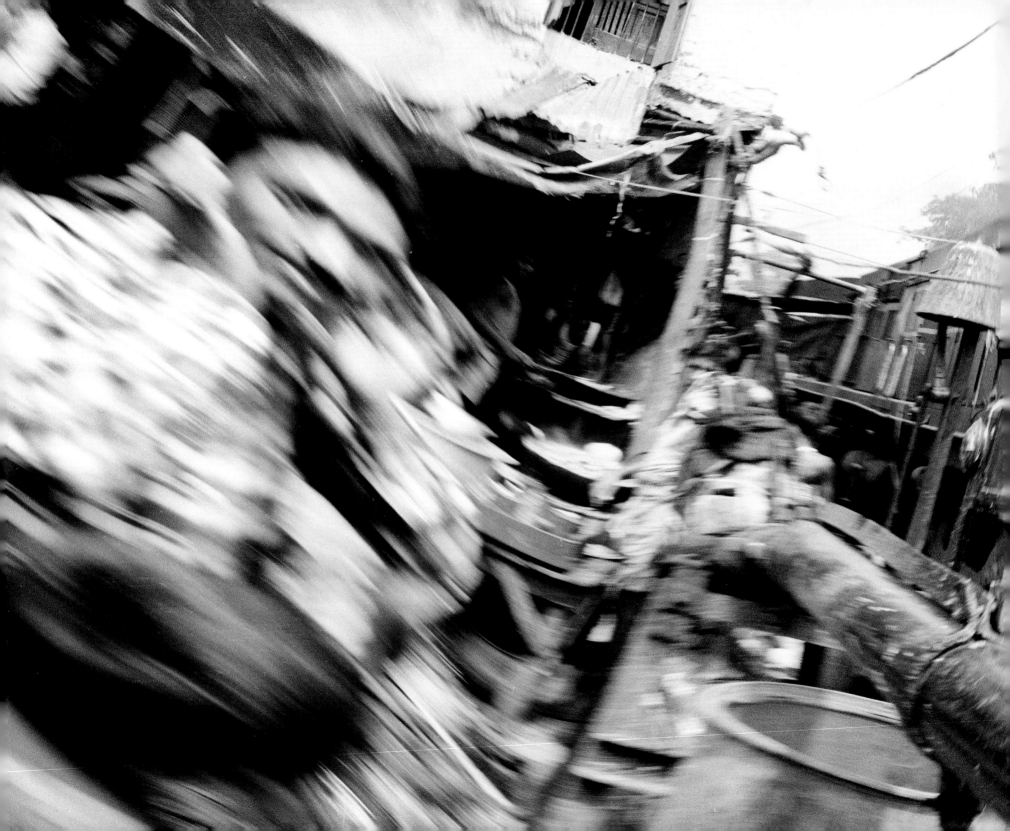

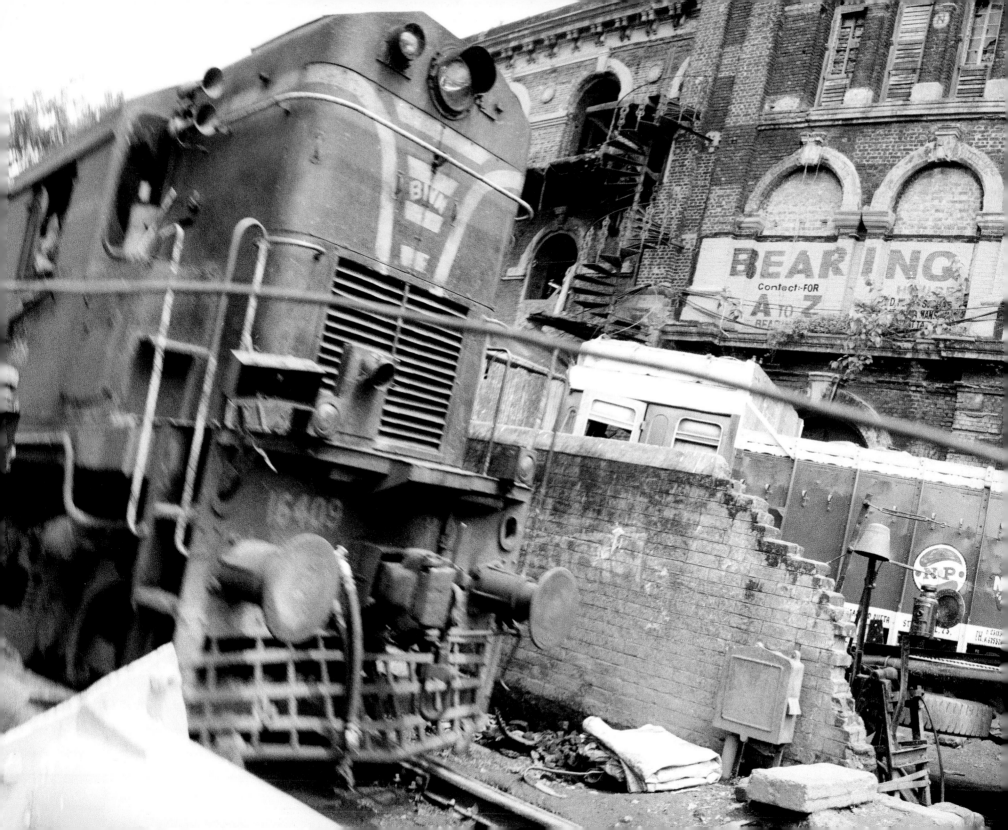

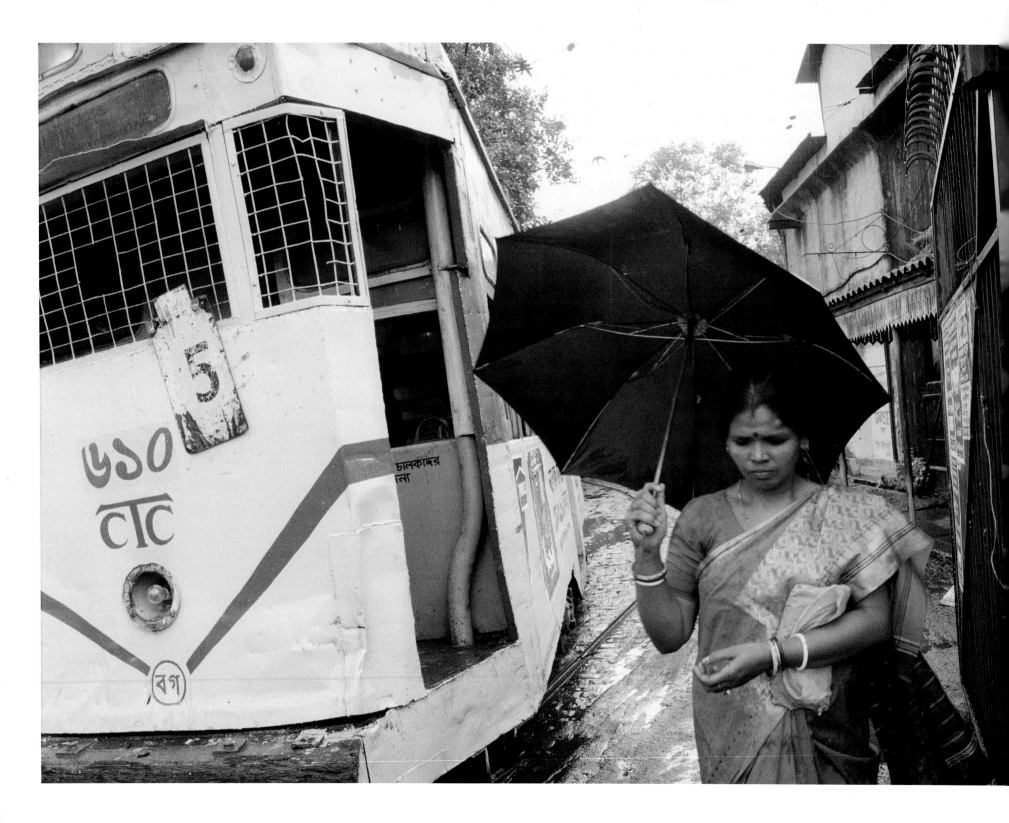

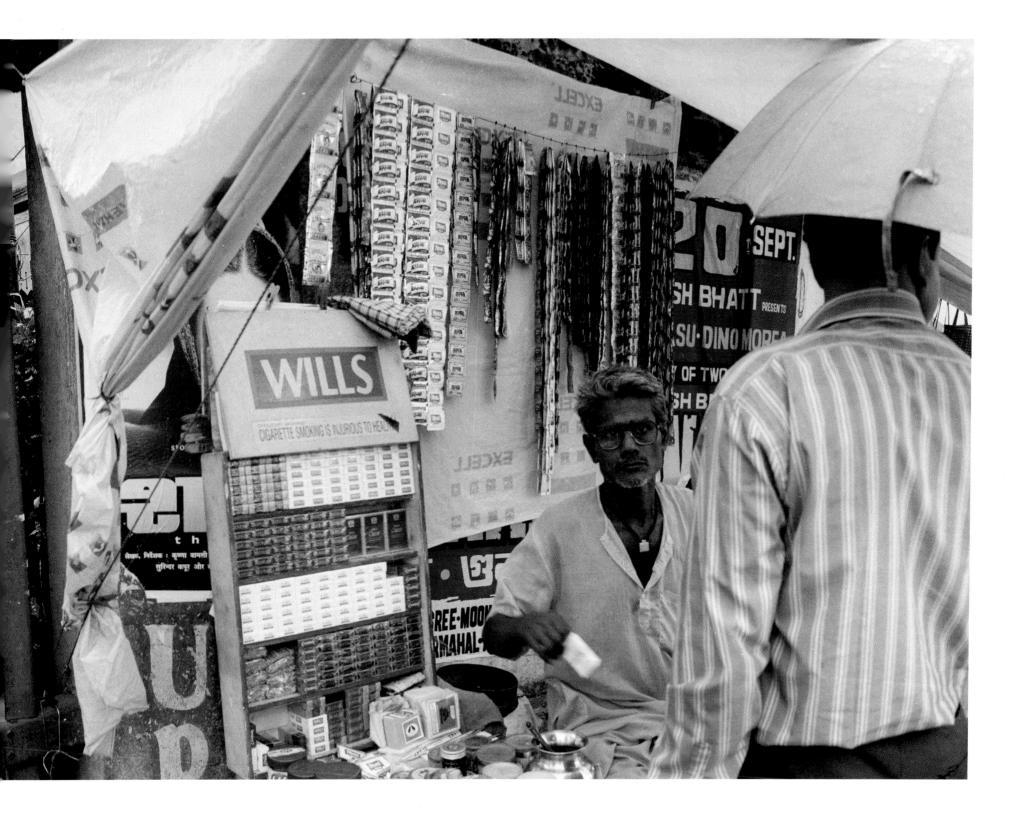

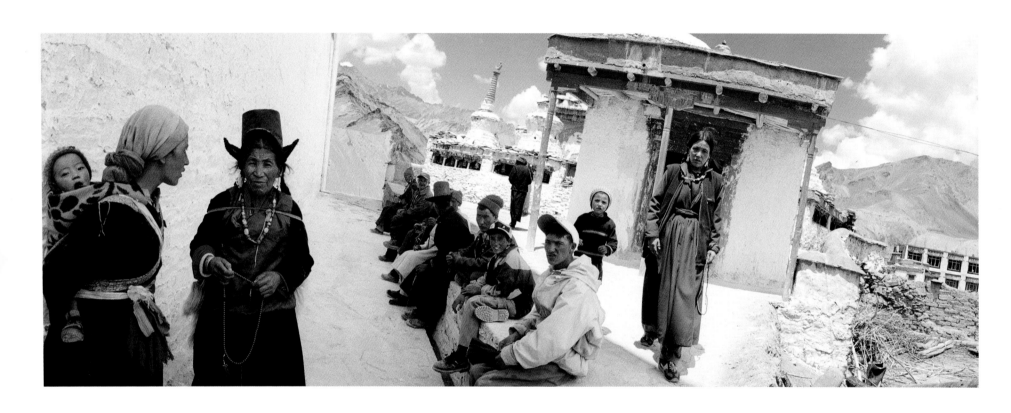

◁ Kolkata, Tram and Umbrella, 2003
Khalsi, Ladakh, Pilgrims, 2000

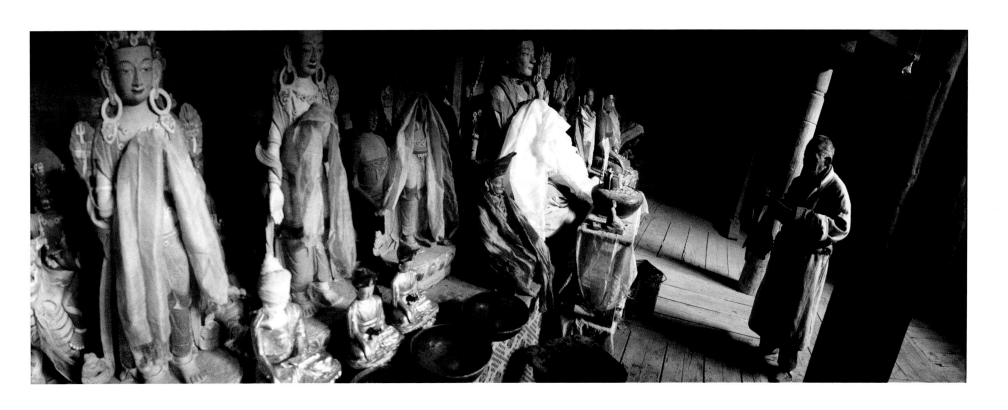

Khalsi, Ladakh, Monastery, 2000
Madurai, Crossroad, 2000 ▷

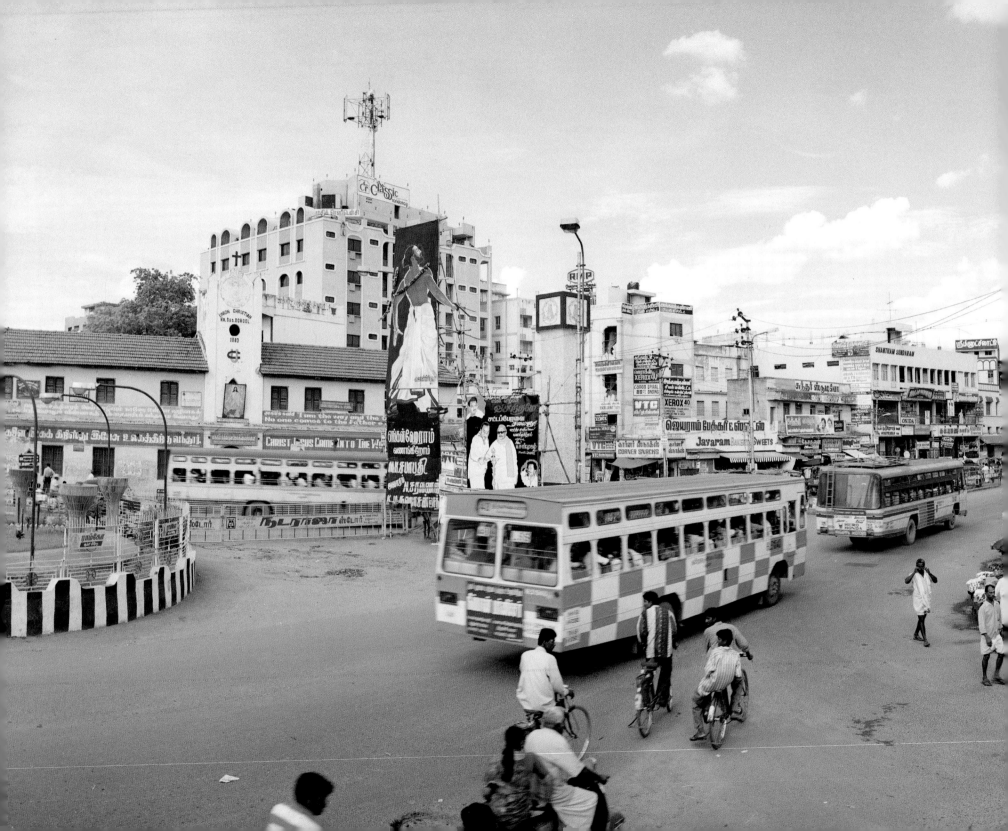

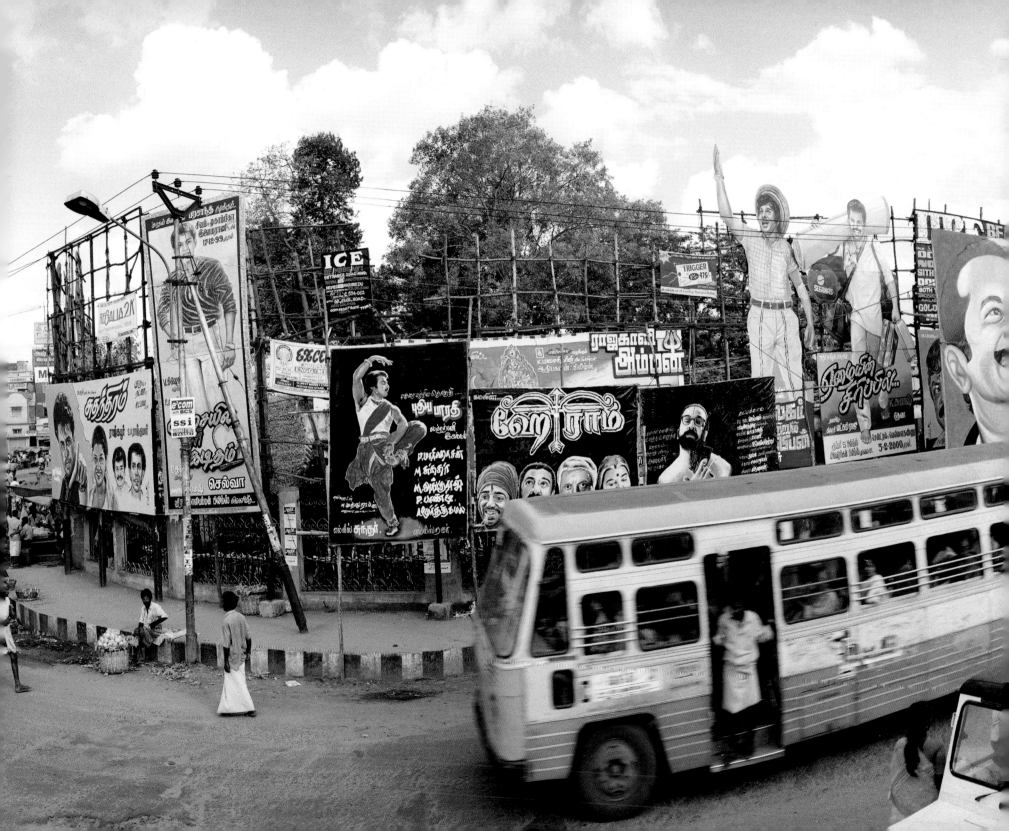

Mammallapuram, Blue Eyes, 1999

This picture was taken for its unreal background;
the bright colors worn by the mother; and the
blue eyes of the boy, all in the middle of nowhere.
Once I'd taken the shot, I got a reality check:
the boy could neither hear nor speak.

Cette image a été prise pour son contexte irréel :
les couleurs vives portées par la mère et les yeux
bleus de l'enfant, le tout au milieu de nulle part.
La photographie prise, retour à la réalité ;
le garçon était sourd et muet.

Questa foto è stata scattata anche per lo sfondo
irreale, i colori brillanti indossati dalla madre e gli
occhi azzurri del bambino nel bel mezzo del nulla.
Poi lo scontro con la realtà: il piccolo era
sordomuto.

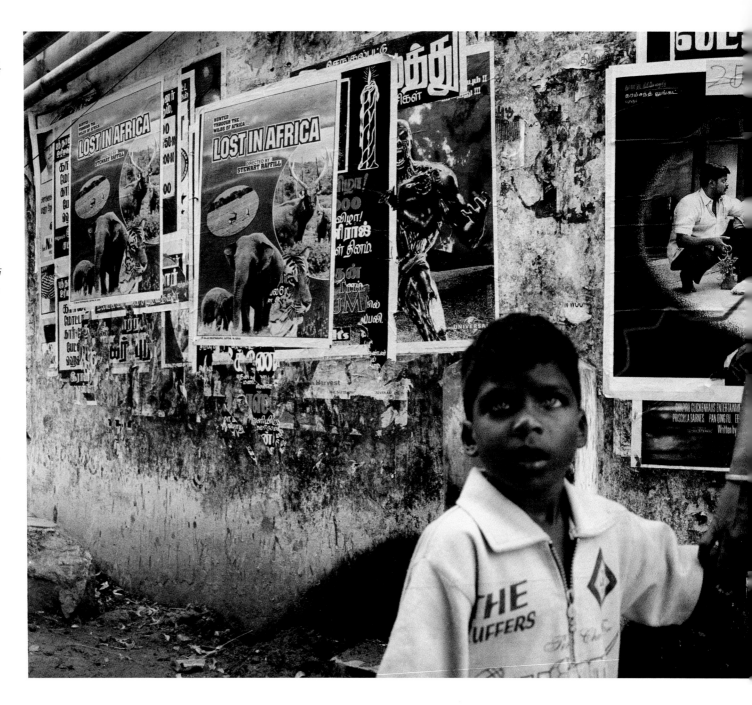

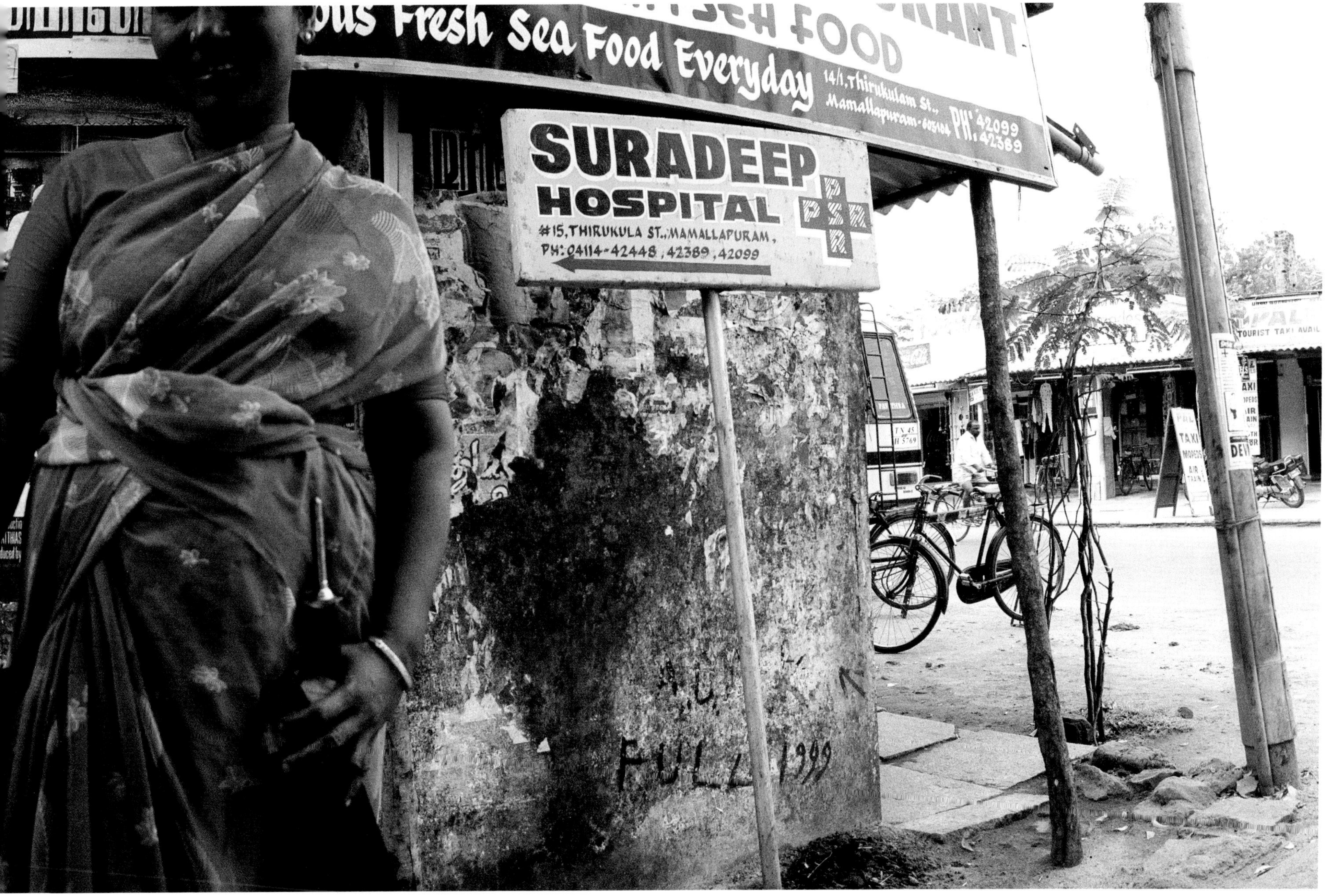
Fresh Sea Food Everyday
14/1, Thirukulam St.,
Mamallapuram-603104
PH: 42099
42389
SURADEEP
HOSPITAL
#15, THIRUKULA ST., MAMALLAPURAM,
PH: 04114-42448, 42389, 42099
FULL 1999
TAXI

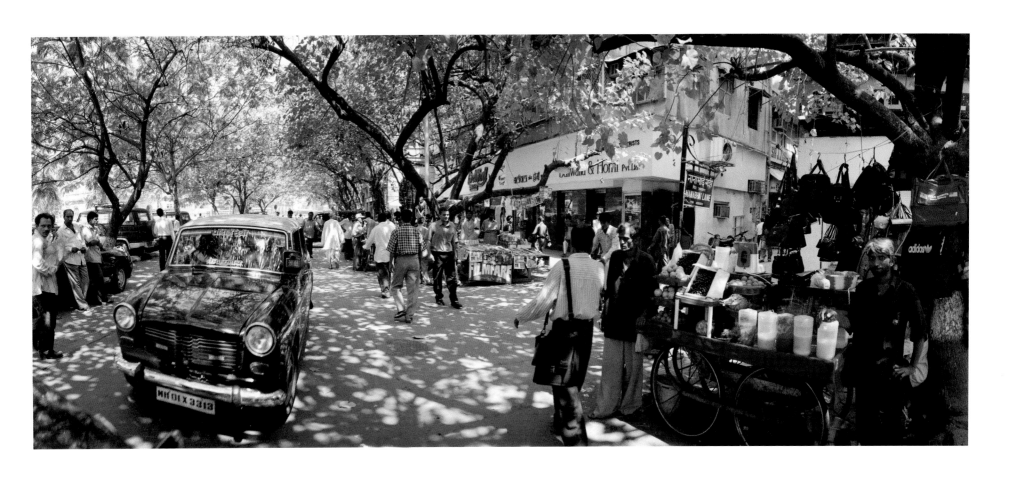

Mumbai, Shadows, 2002

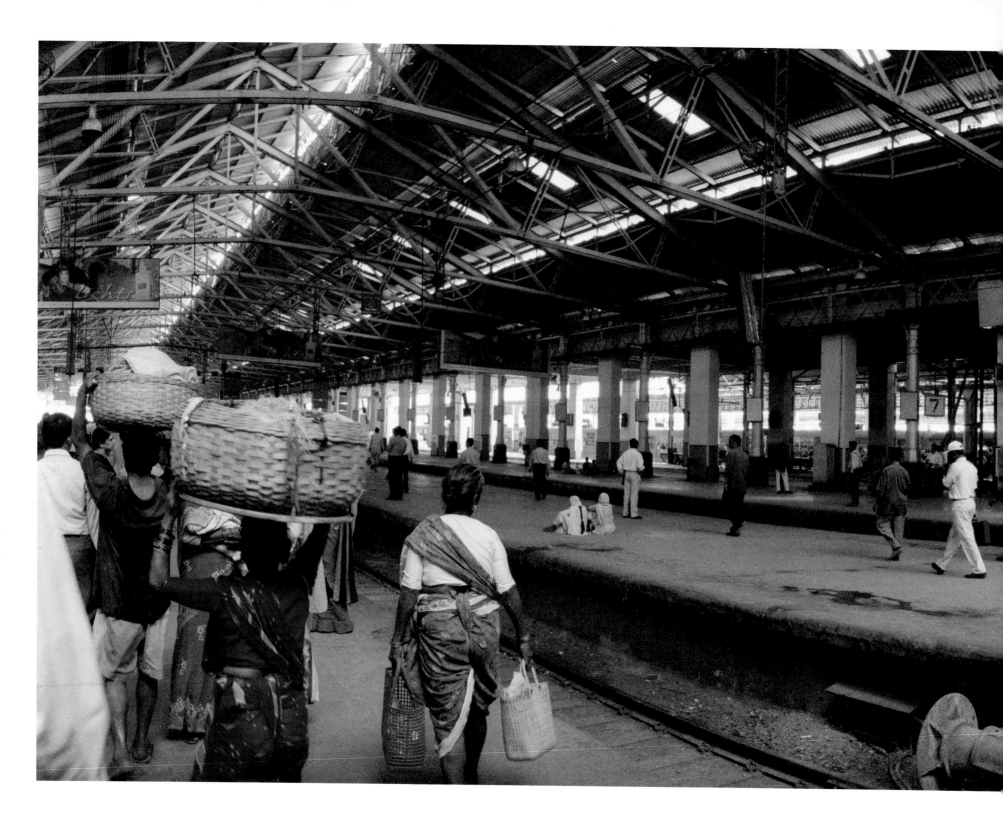

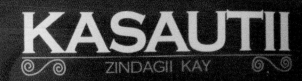

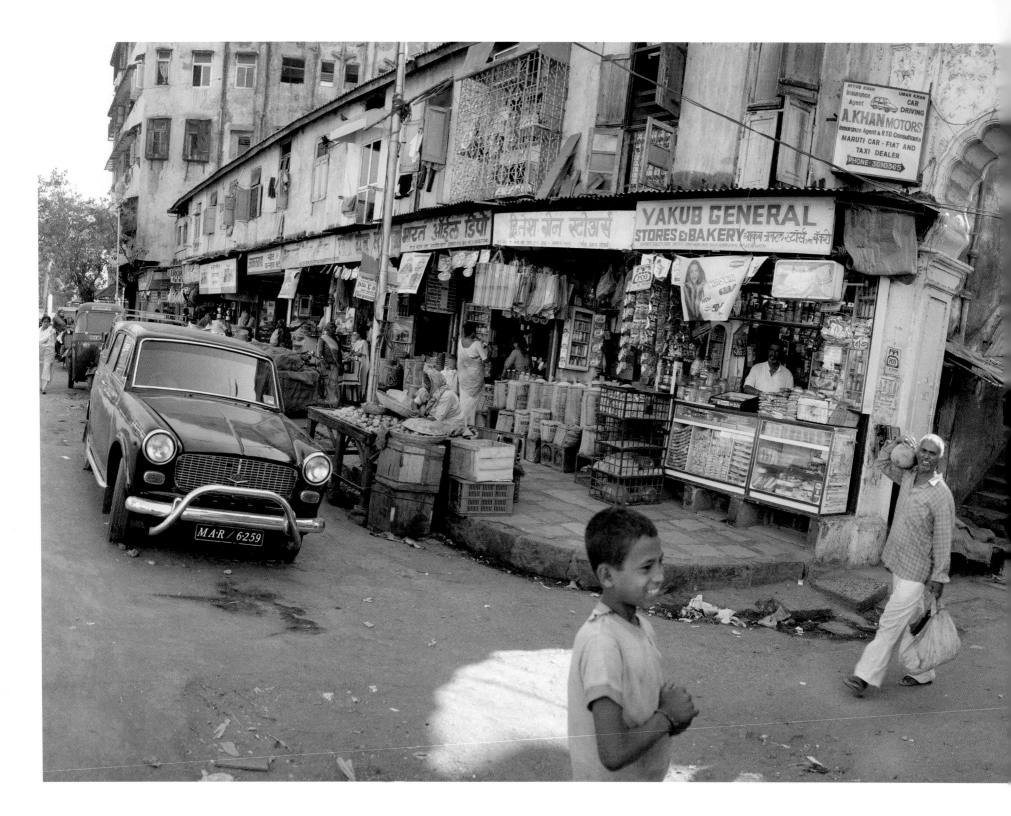

◁◁ Mumbai, Train Station, 2002

Mumbai, Old City Door, 2002

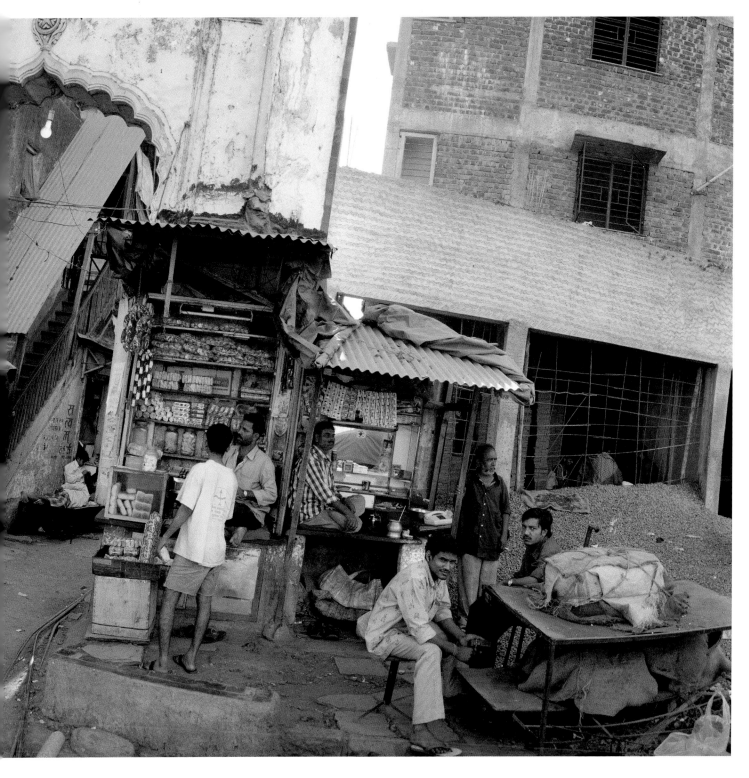

Mumbai, Beach Attractions, 2001 ▷

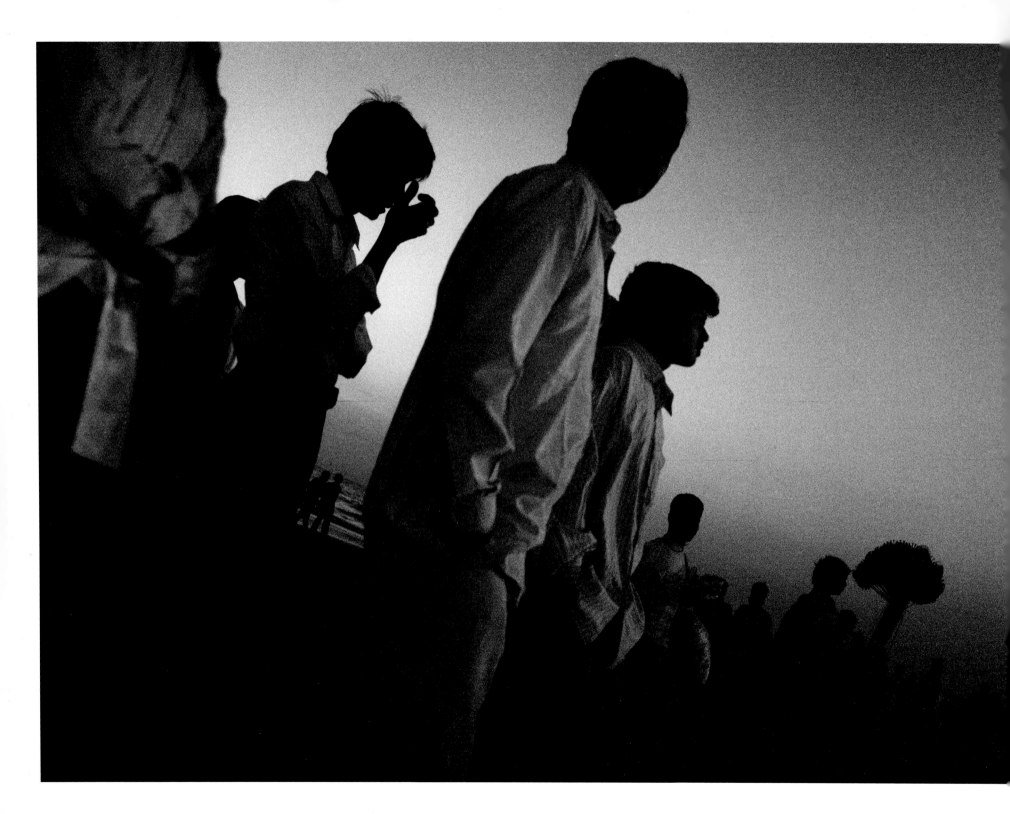

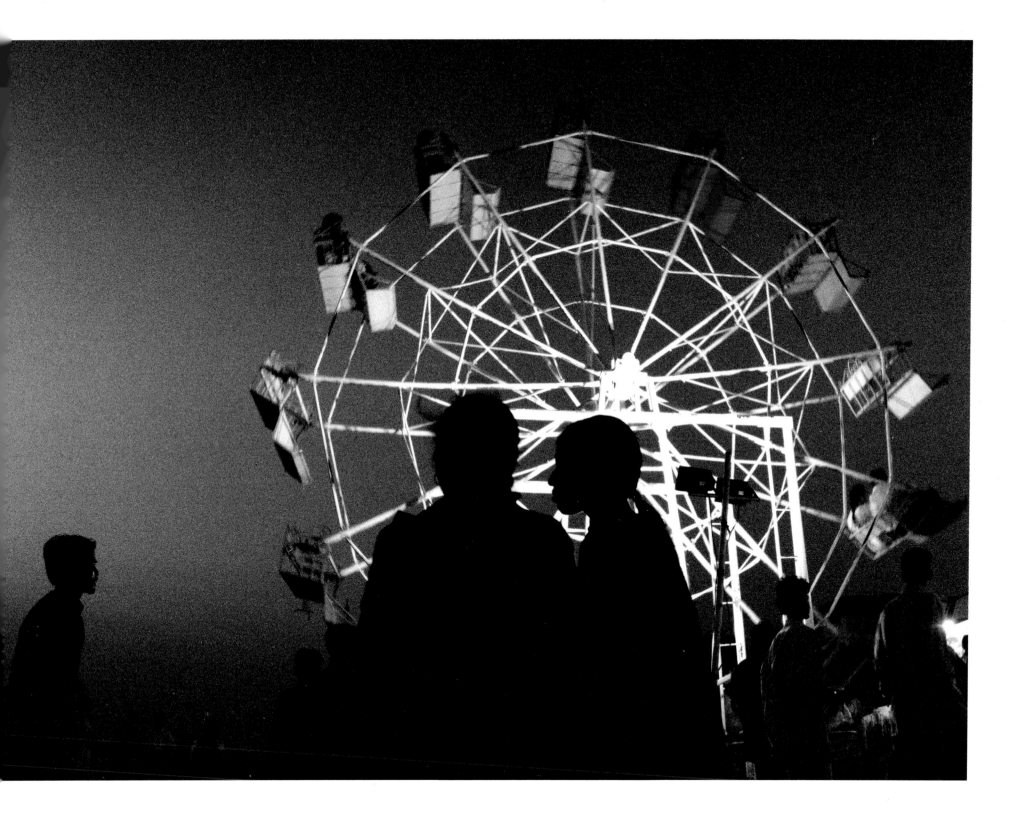

Mussoorie, Shopping Street, 2001

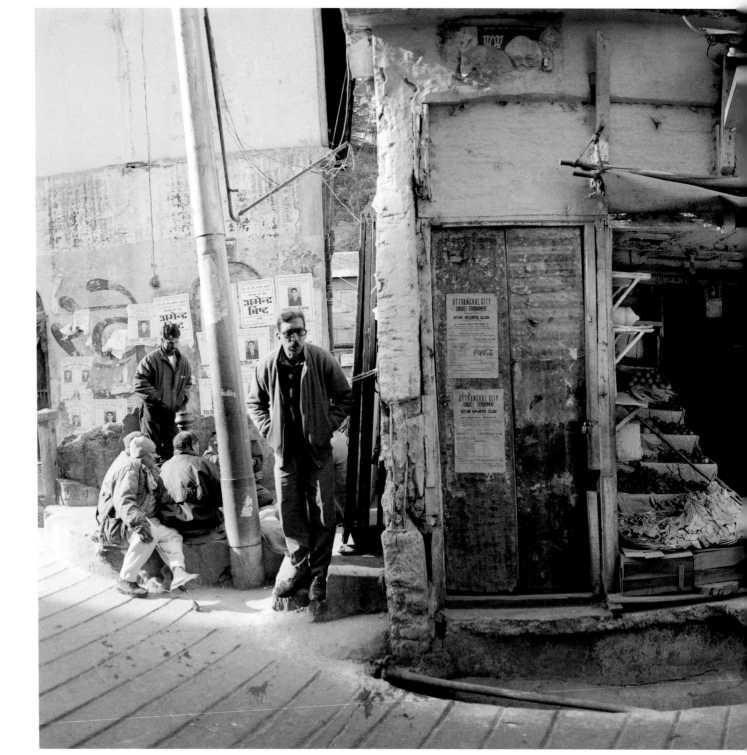

Orissa, Washing Plates in the River, 2001 ▷▷

Panaji, Barbershop, 2001 ▷▷

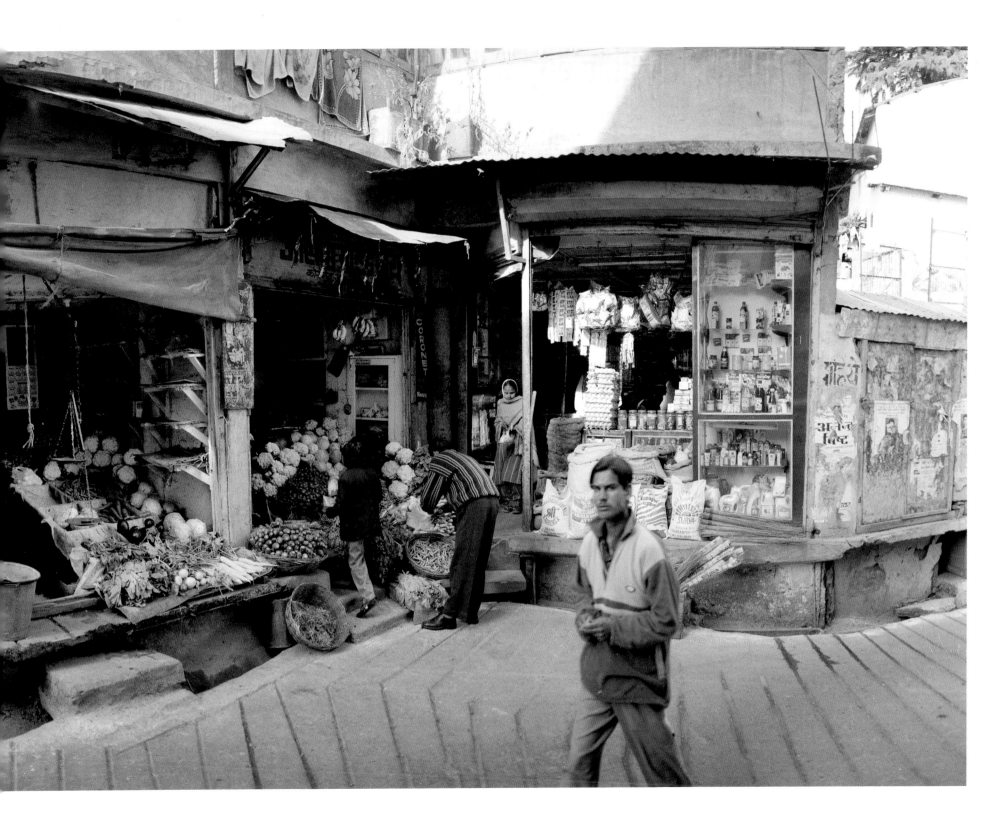

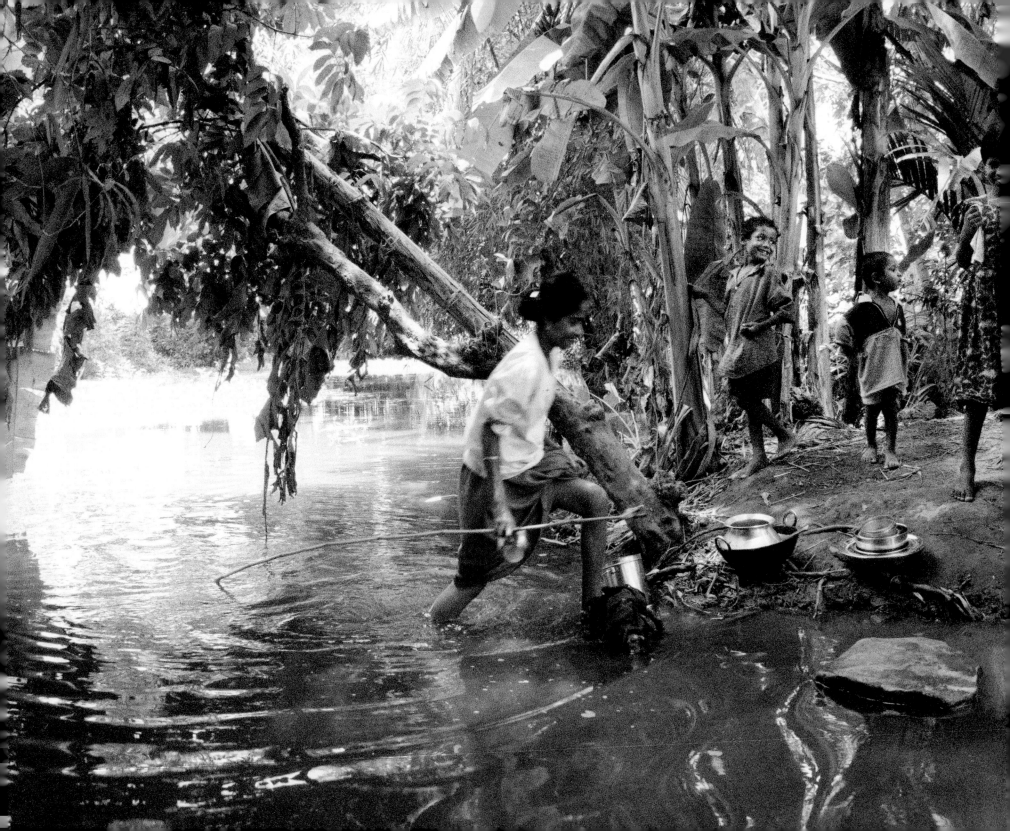

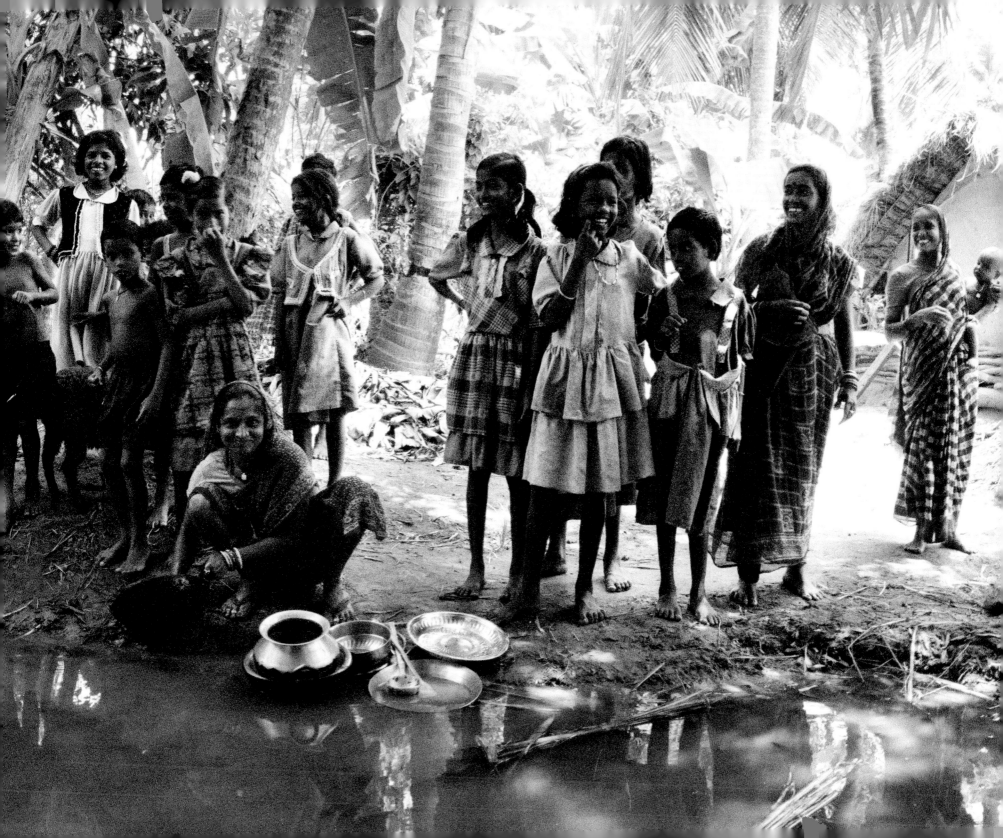

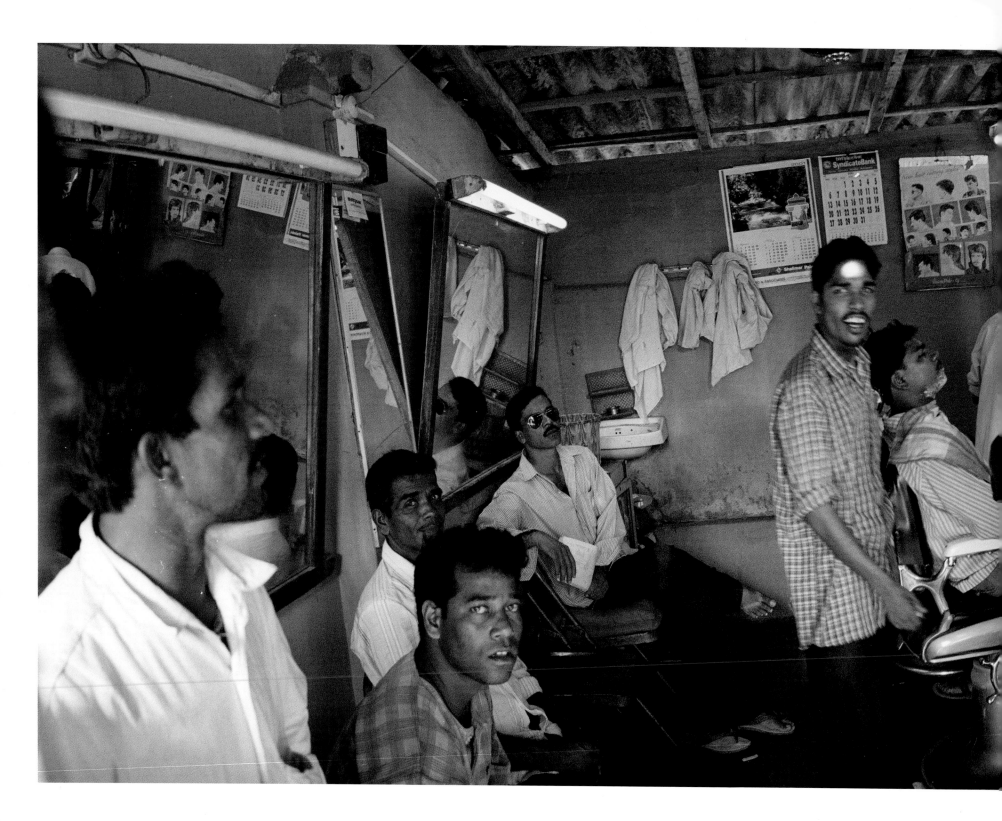

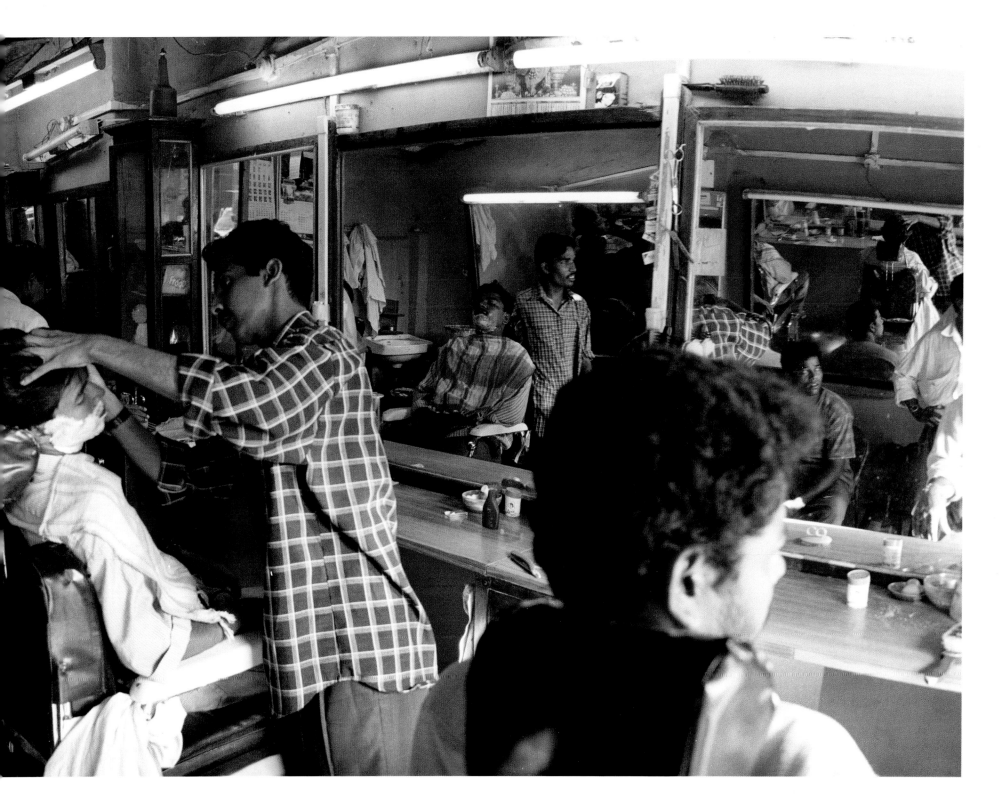

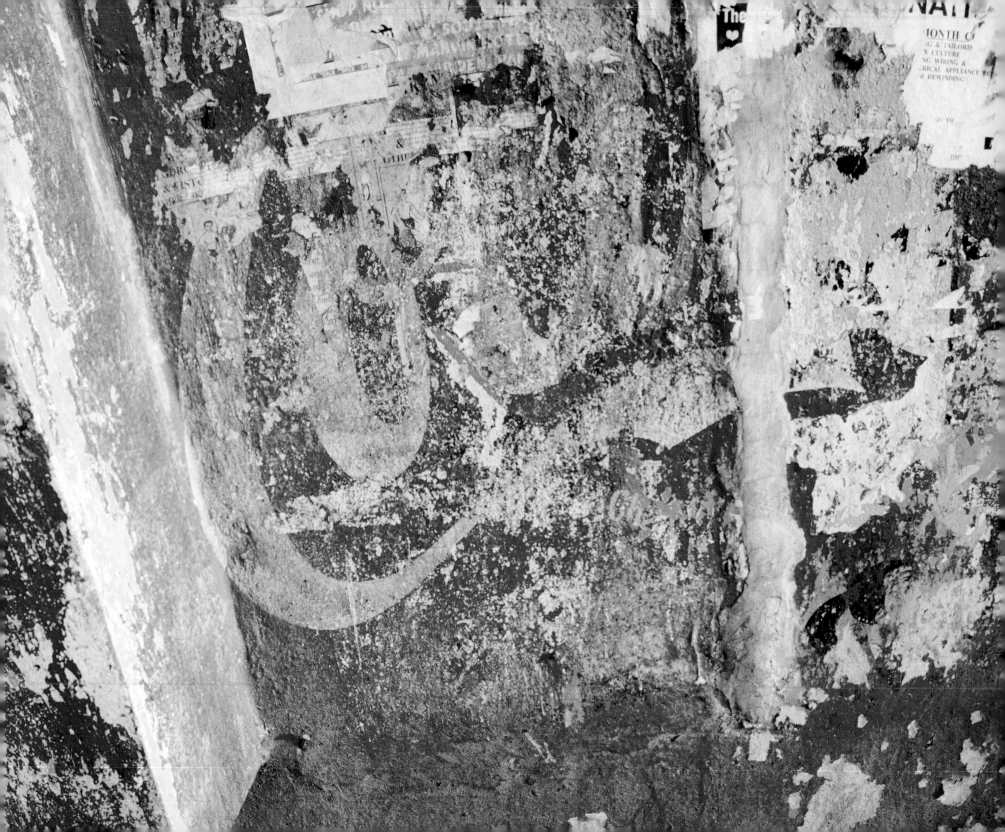

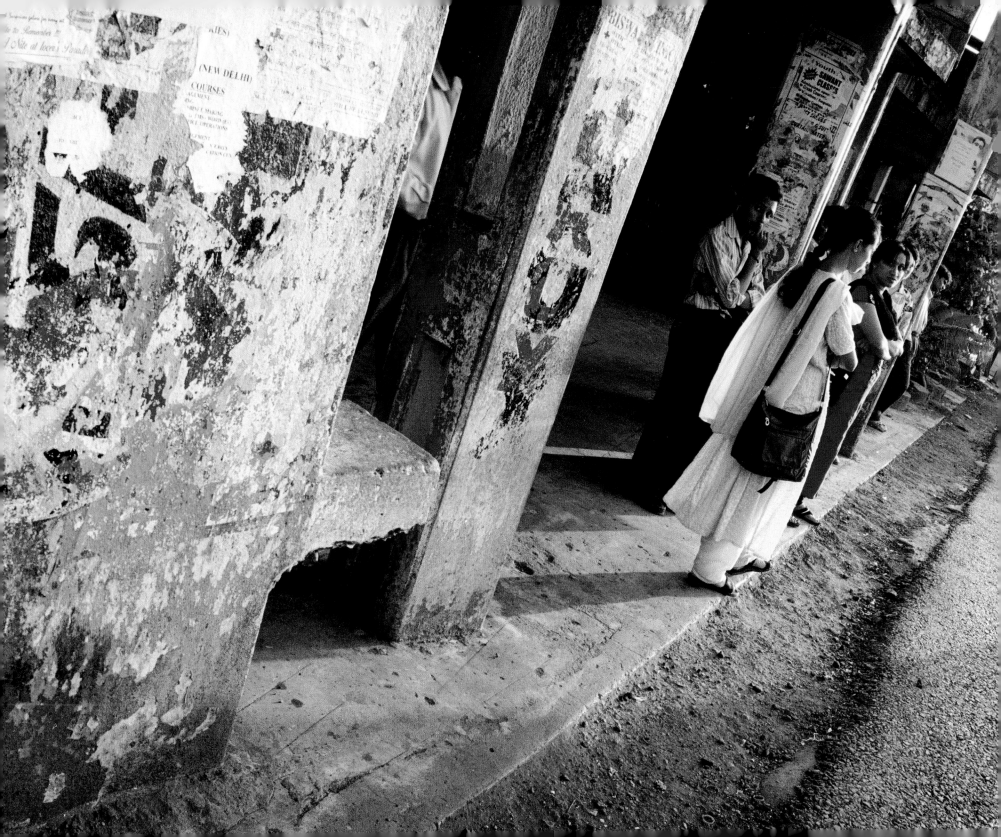

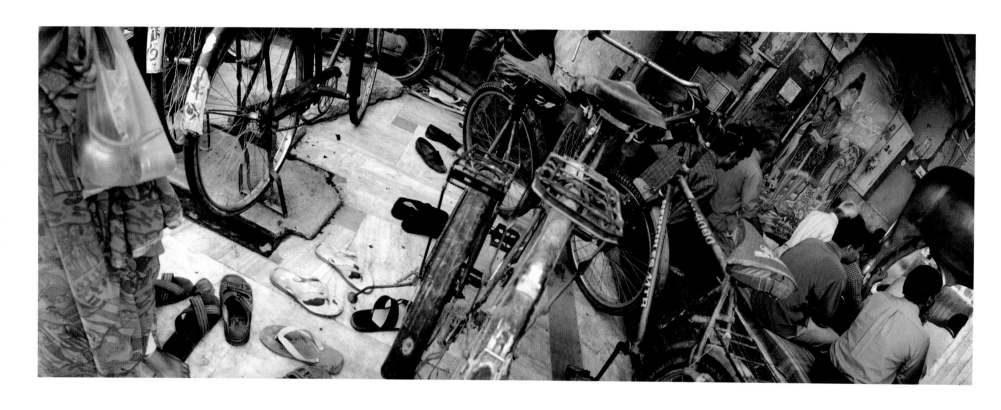

◁ Panaji, The Wall, 2002
Udaipur, Near the Temple, 2002

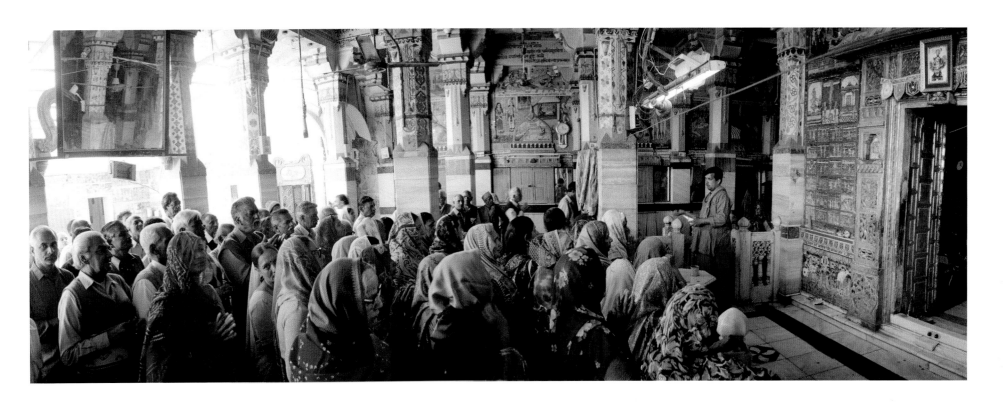

Rajasthan, Prayer, 2002

Puri, Legal Center, 2002

In the middle of a small town lawyers and consultants offer their services from an unusual office complex.

Au milieu d'une petite ville, des avocats et des consultants juridiques offrent leurs services dans un complexe de bureaux plutôt inhabituel.

Al centro di una piccola città, avvocati e consulenti legali offrono i loro servizi in un ufficio piuttosto inusuale.

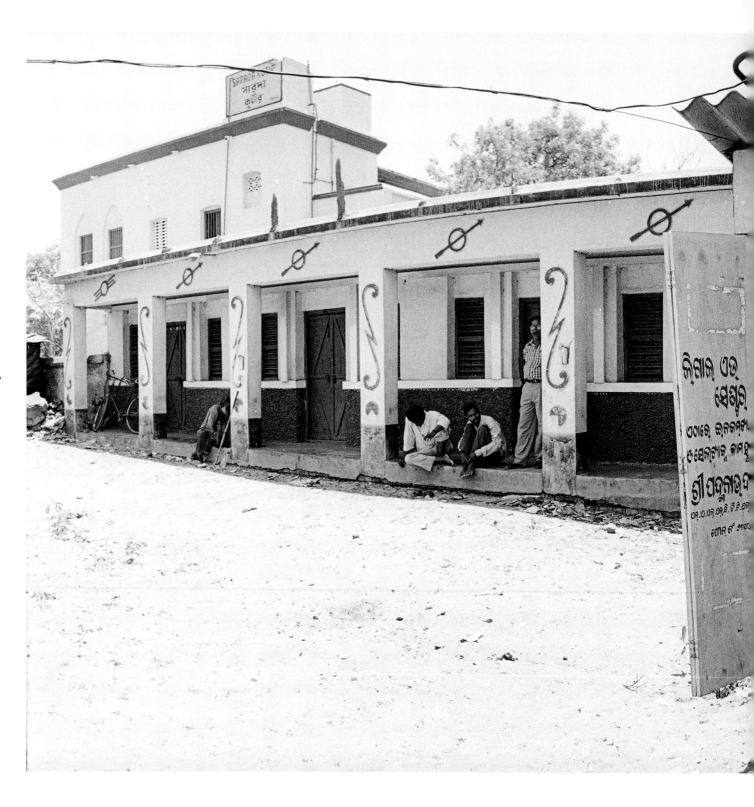

Puri, Beach Photographers, 2002 ▷▷

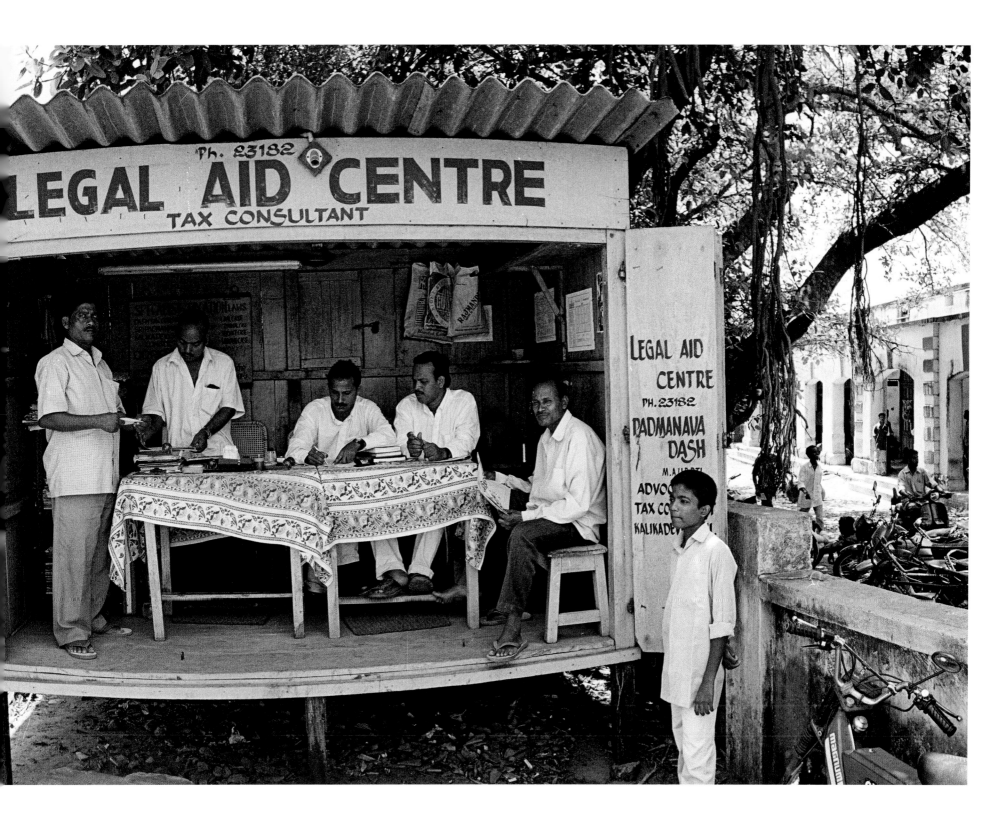

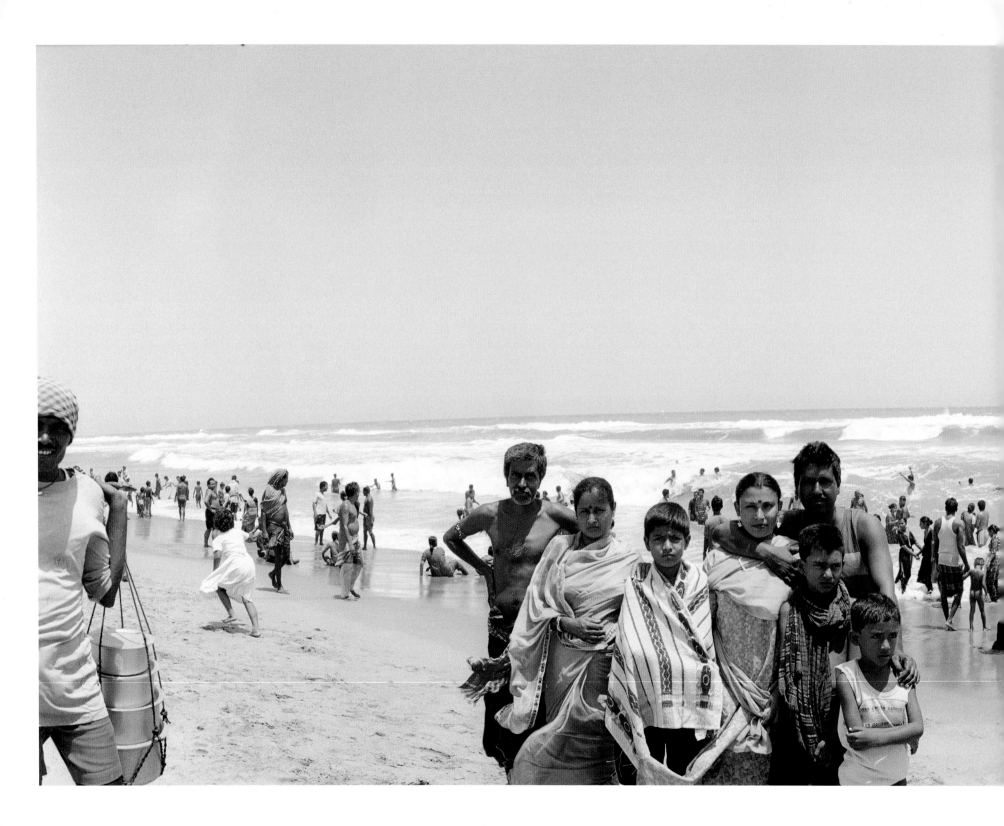

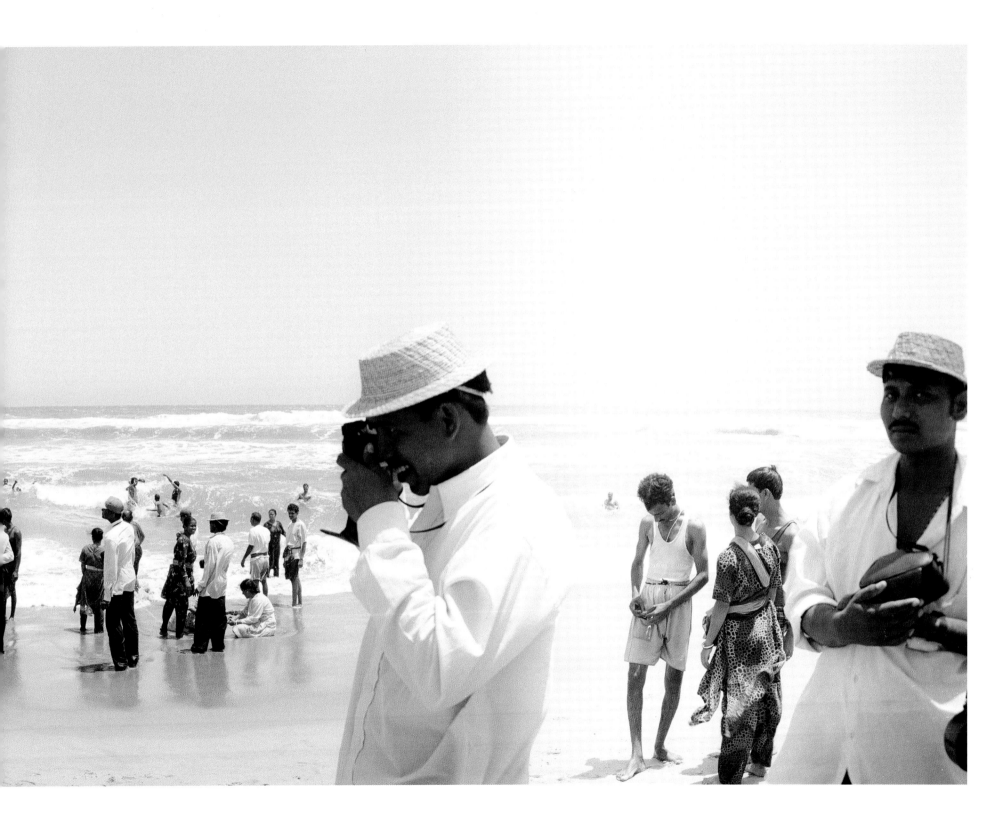

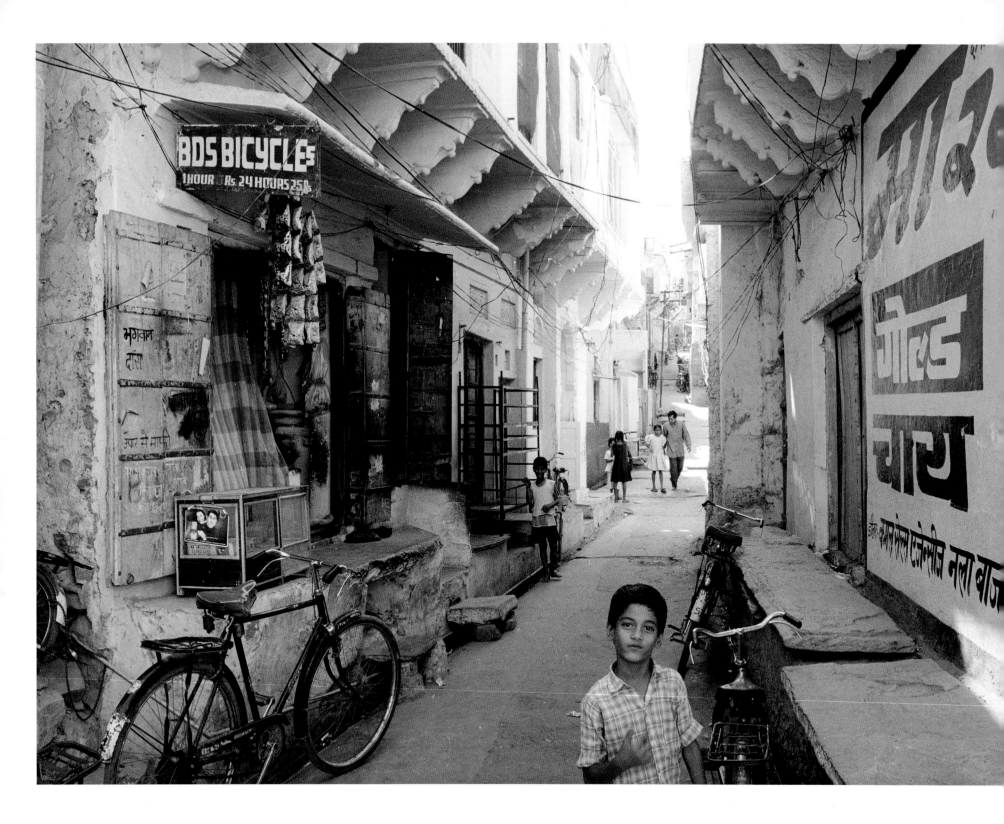

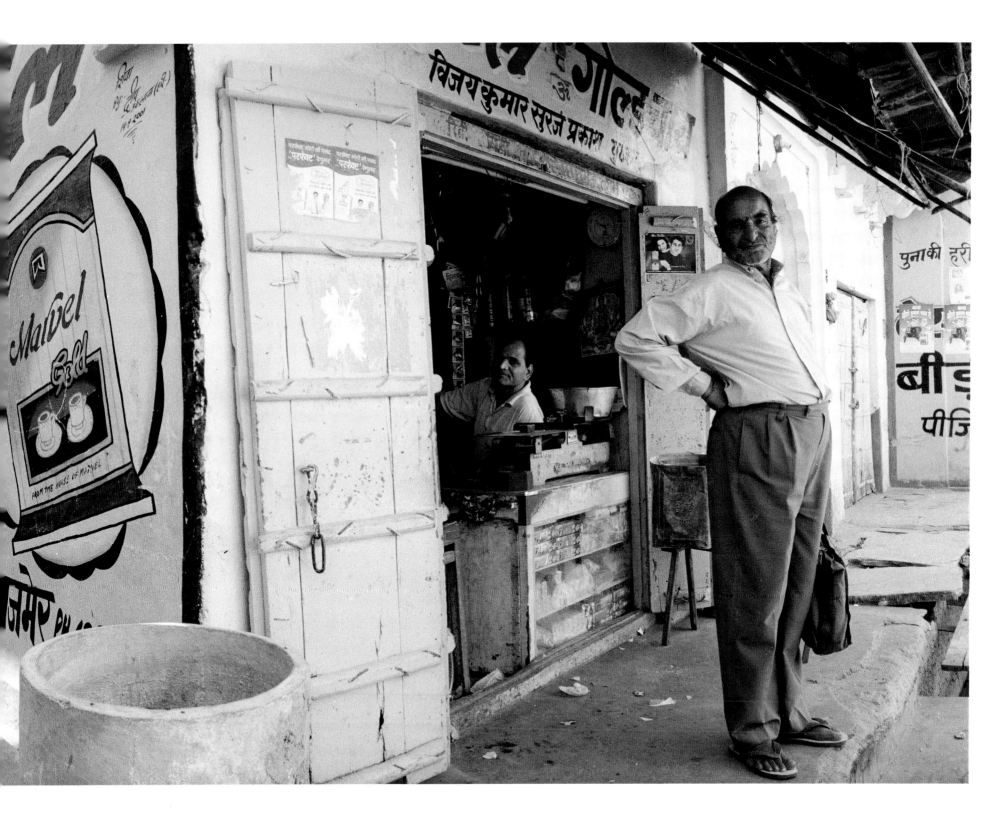

◁ Puskar, Contentment, 2002

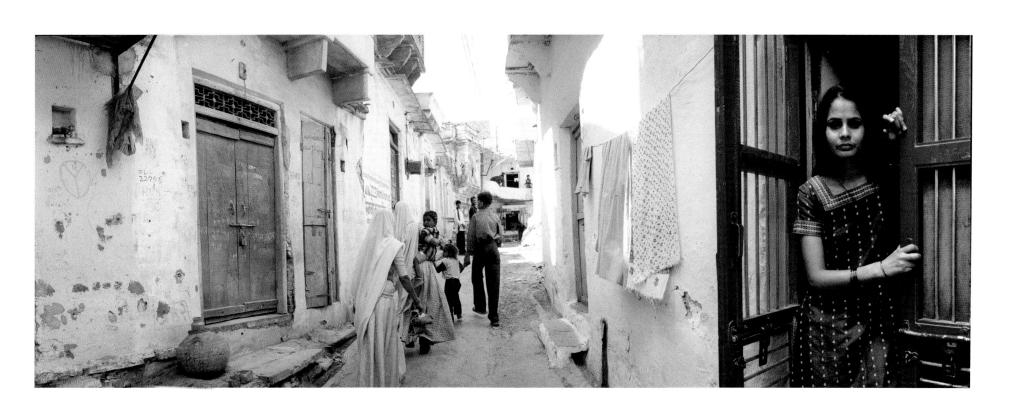

Puskar, Girl in the Door, 2002

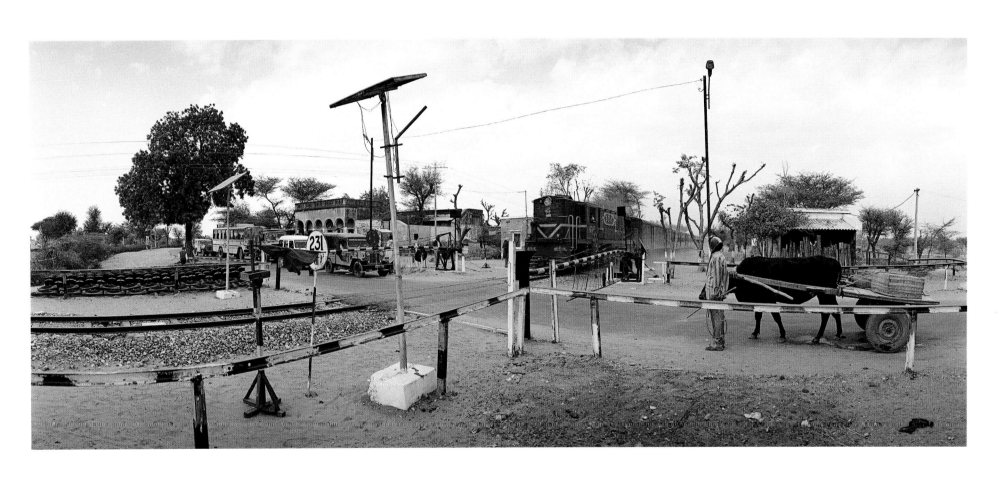

Rajasthan, Train Passage, 2001

Rajasthan, Village Board, 2002

*After the death of an important villager, men
gather in a council to deliberate on his succession.
Grouped together, women await the outcome.*

*Après la mort d'un important villageois,
les hommes se réunissent en conseil pour délibérer
de sa succession. Réunies, les femmes attendent
leurs décisions.*

*Dopo la morte di un importante abitante del
villaggio, gli uomini si riuniscono in assemblea per
discuterne la successione. Le donne attendono
insieme l'esito.*

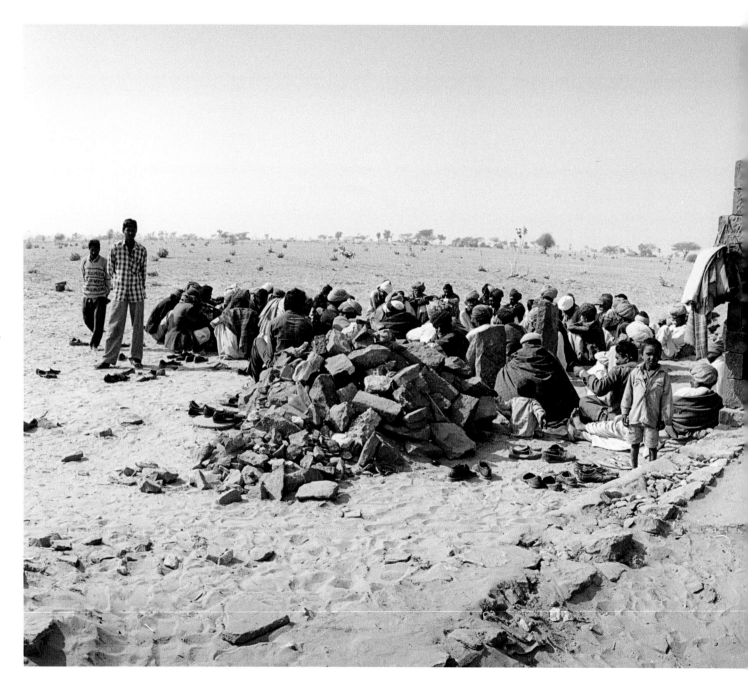

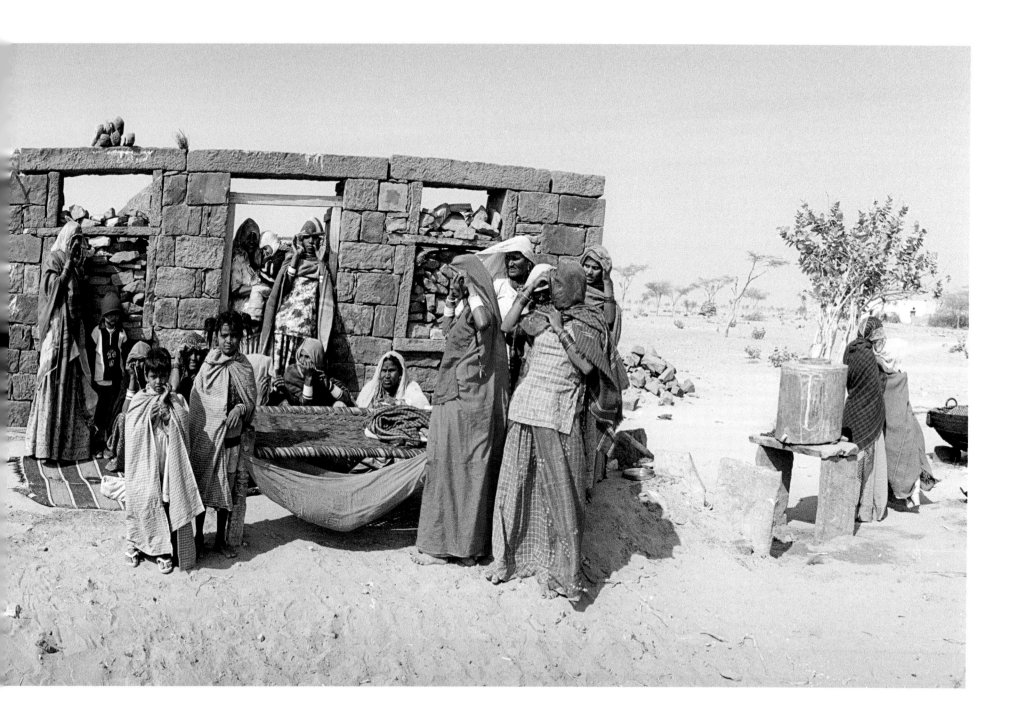

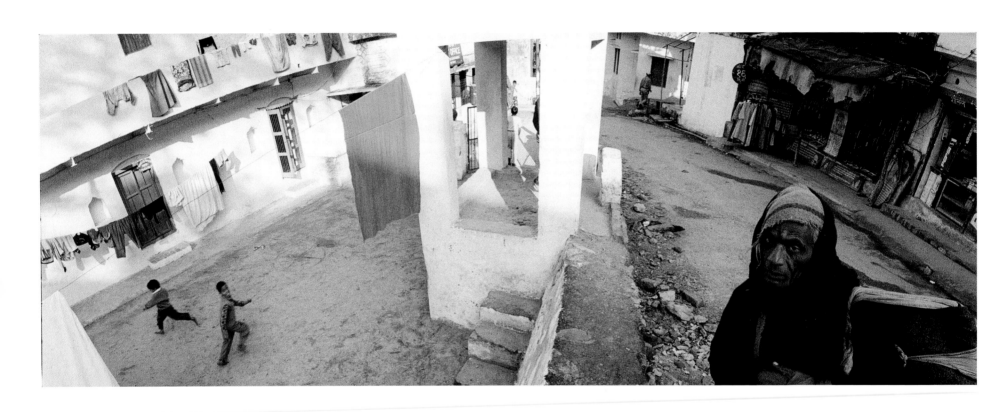

Rishikesh, Kids Playing with Photographer, 2000

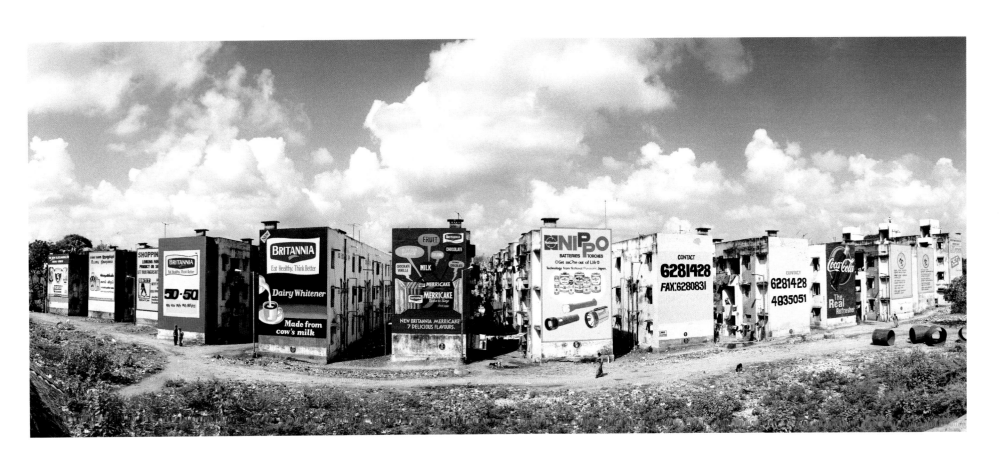

Chennai, Advertisements, 2000

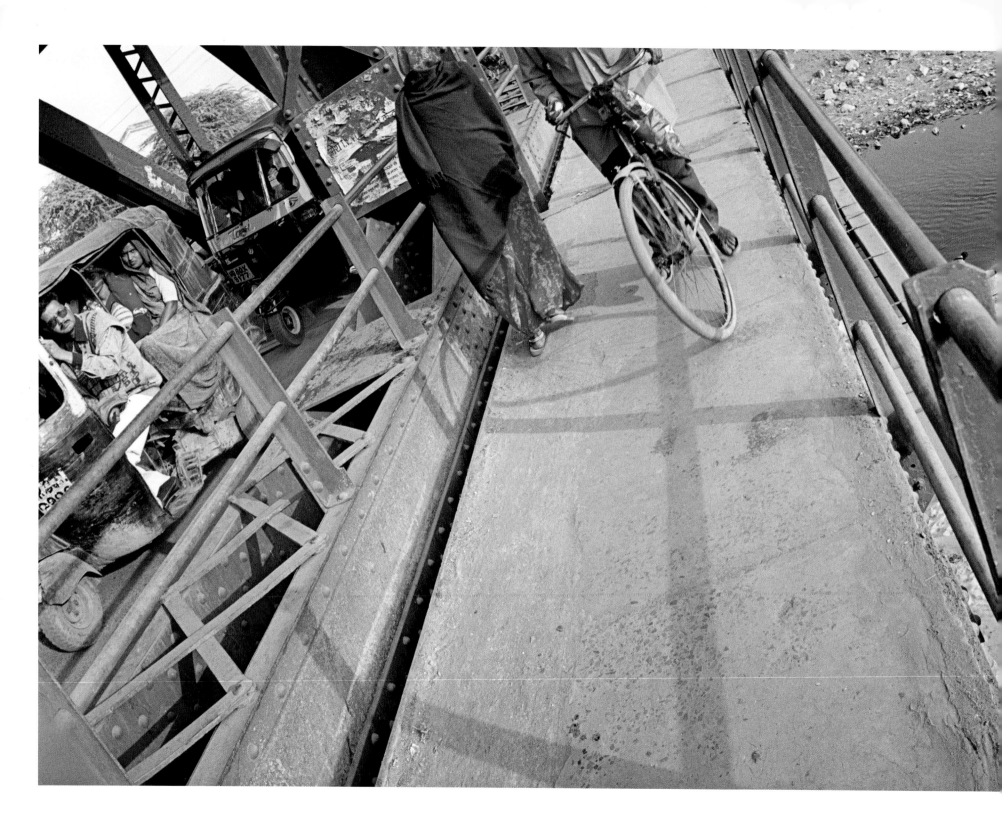

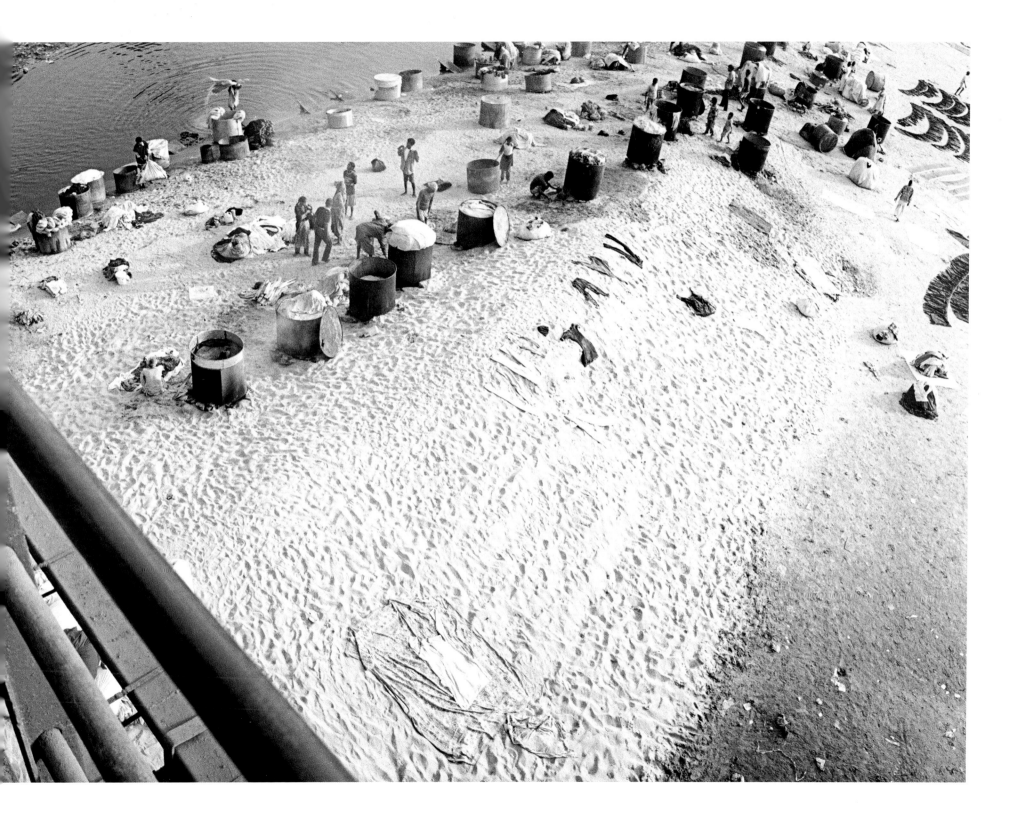

◁ Agra, Laundry, 2002

Agra, Taj Mahal, 2002

The Taj Mahal is the most-photographed
monument in India, and it is not easy to avoid
repeating others. In this shot the monument is
behind me, but one can still appreciate its
beauty. This may be my most touristy picture,
but then this too is India.

Le Taj Mahal est le monument indien le plus
photographié ; ne pas refaire ce qui a déjà été fait
tant de fois n'est pas facile. Ici, le monument est
derrière moi, mais on peut encore apprécier sa
beauté. C'est peut-être ma photographie la plus
touristique, mais c'est aussi un aspect de l'Inde.

Il Taj Mahal è il monumento più fotografato
dell'India: non è facile fare a meno di ripetersi.
In questo scatto l'edificio è alle mie spalle, tuttavia
se ne percepisce la bellezza. Sarà forse una foto
piuttosto 'turistica', ma anche questa è l'India.

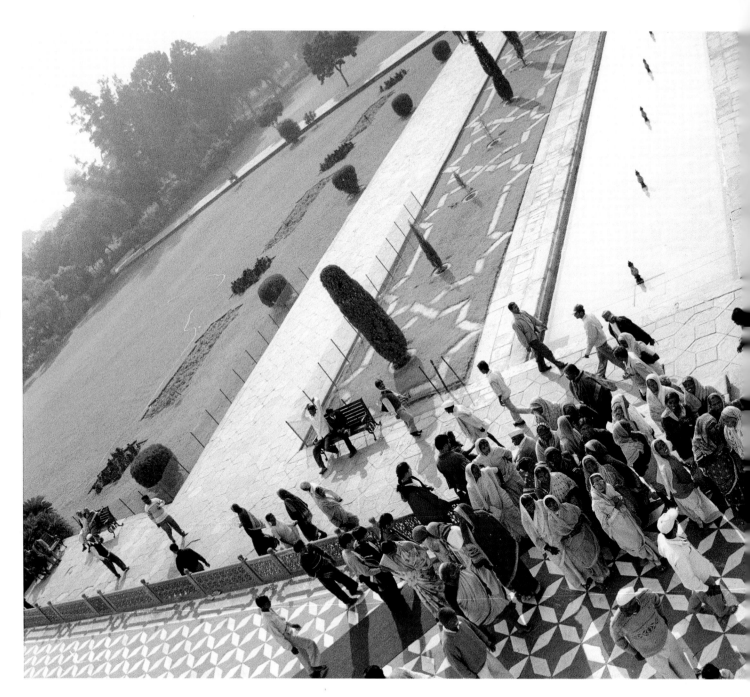

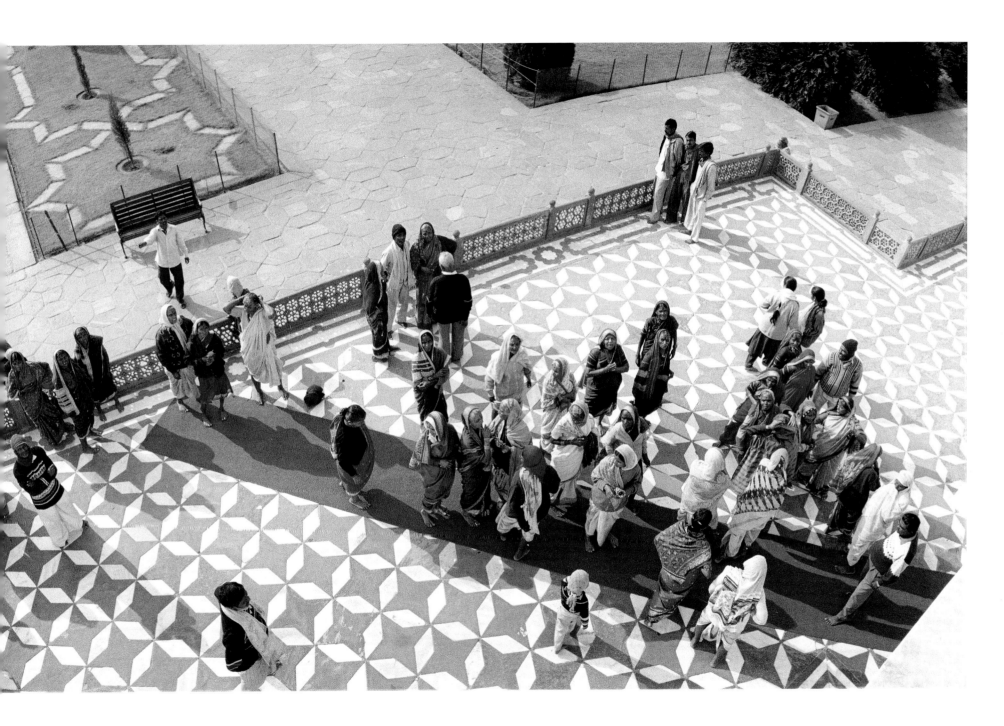

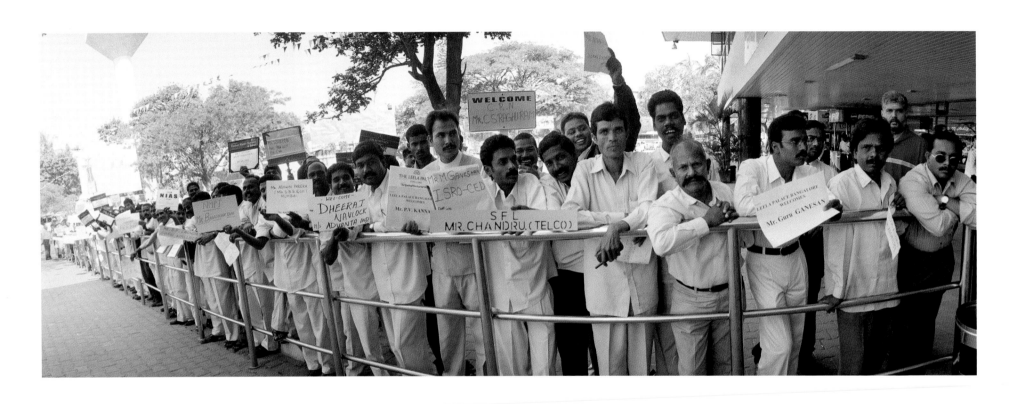

Bangalore, Airport, 2002

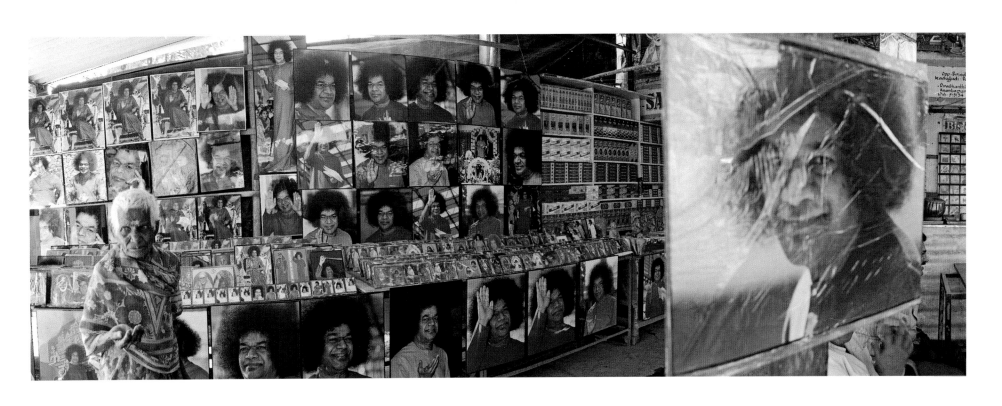

Bangalore, Baba, 2003

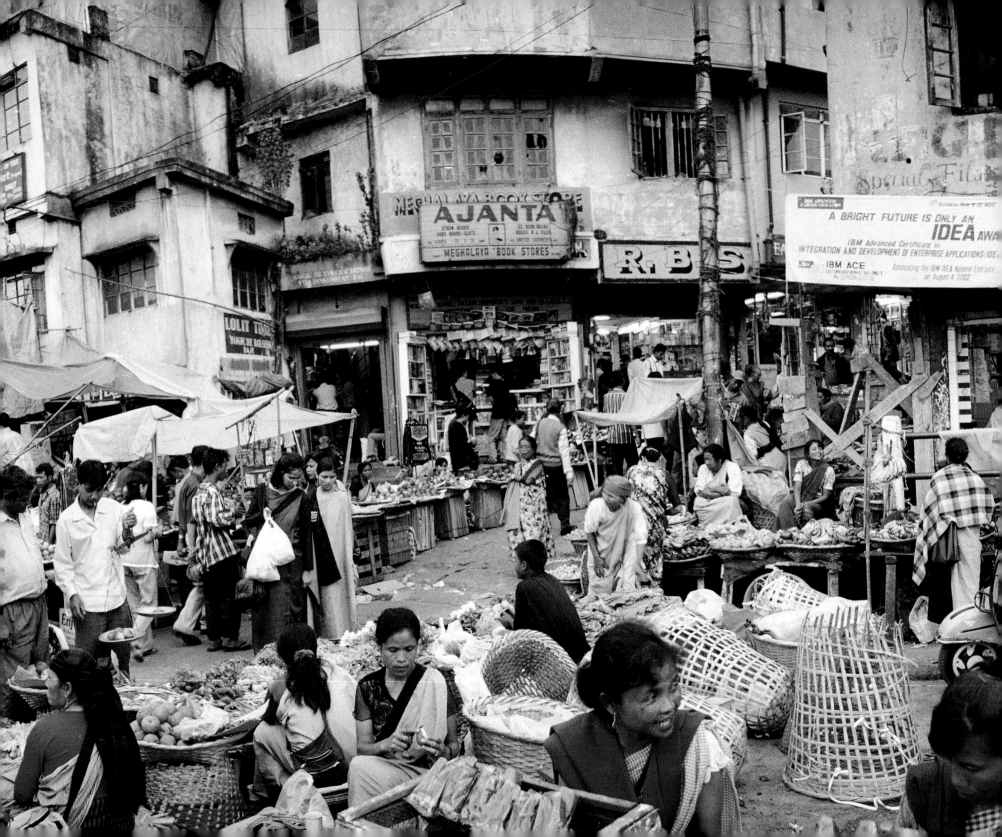

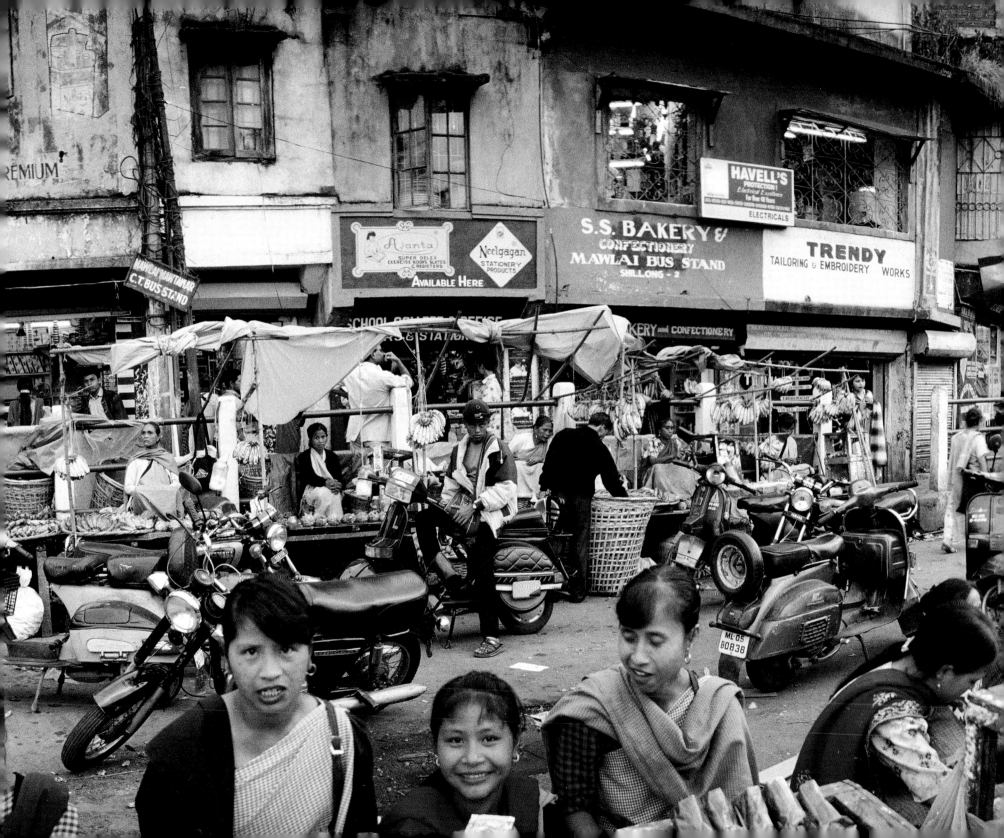

Ajmer, Food Distribution, 2002

In a backstreet of Ajmer, a small and tidy restaurant prepares food to distribute to beggars.

Dans une ruelle d'Ajmer, un petit restaurant très propre où l'on prépare de la nourriture pour la distribuer aux mendiants.

In una strada secondaria di Ajmer, un ristorantino minuscolo e pulito prepara il cibo da distribuire ai mendicanti.

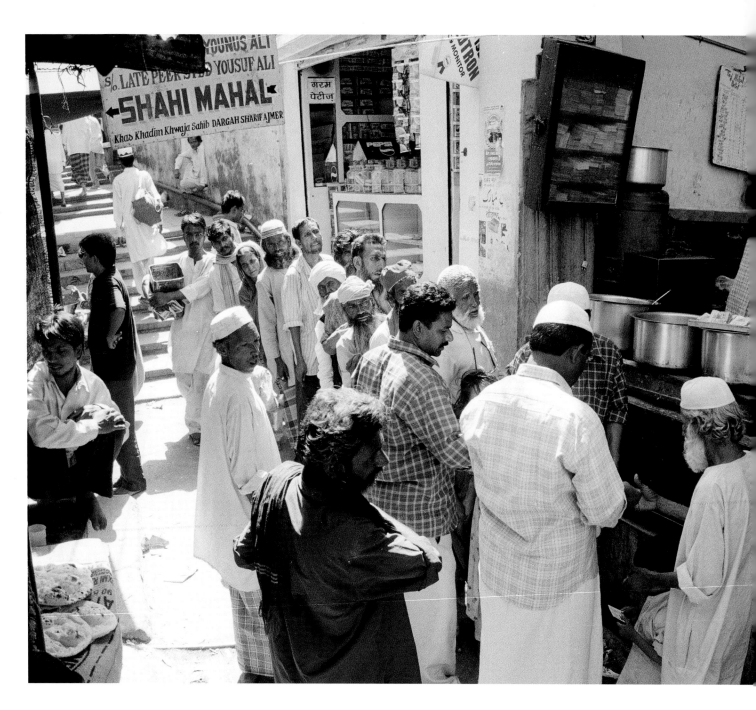

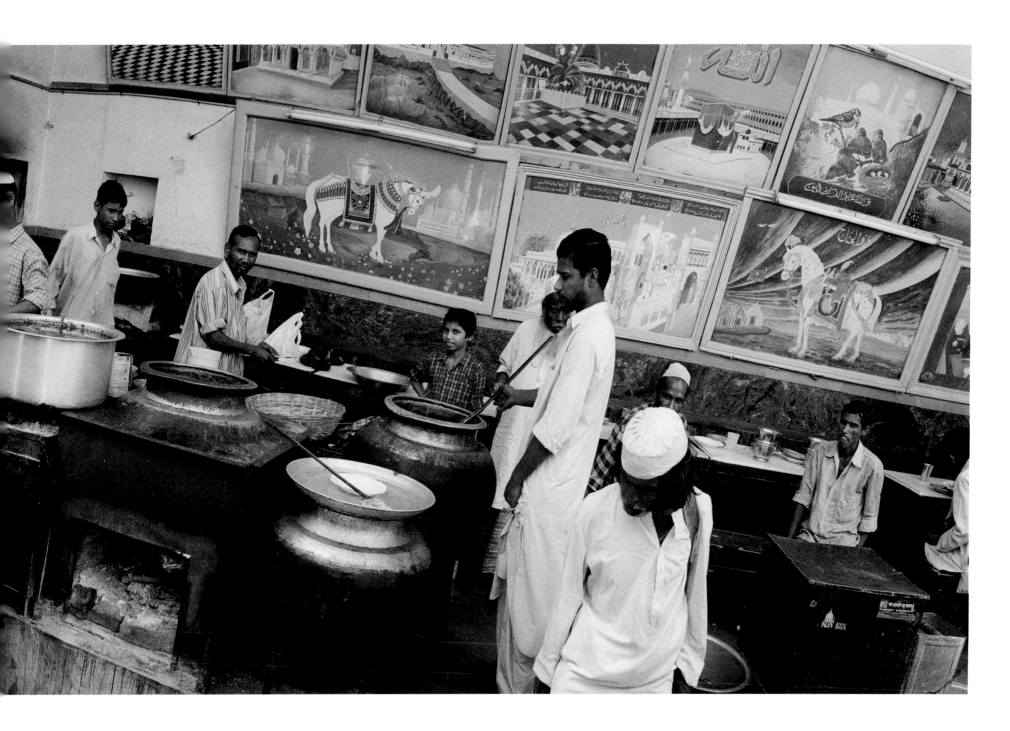

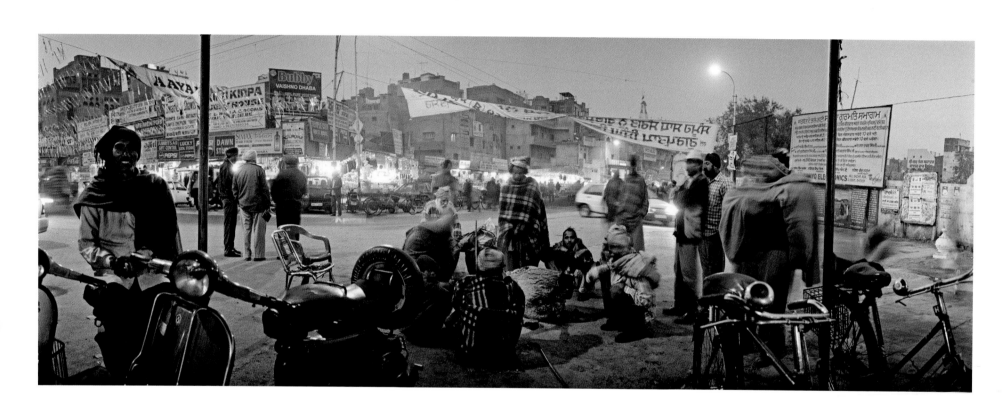

Amritsar, Taxi Drivers Waiting, 2003

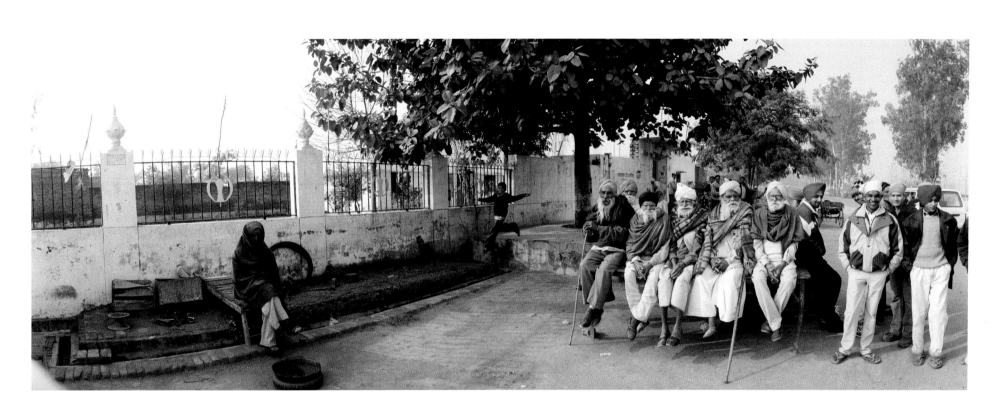

Amritsar, Jump, 2003

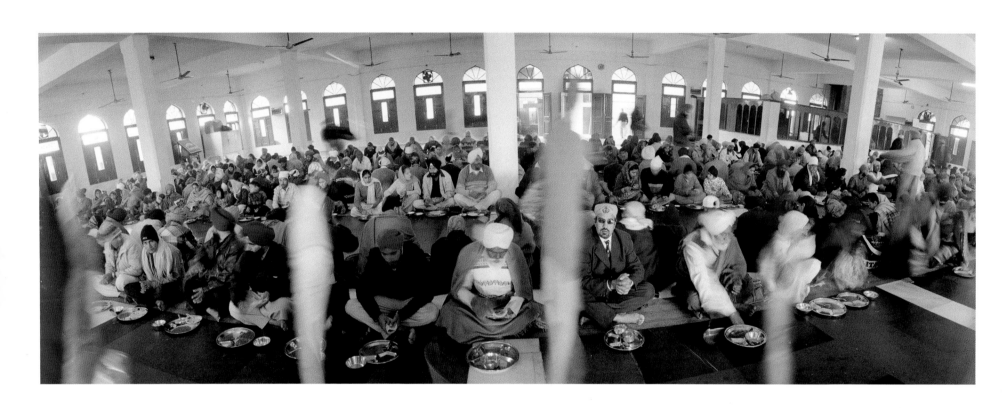

Amritsar, Golden Temple, Food Distribution, 2003

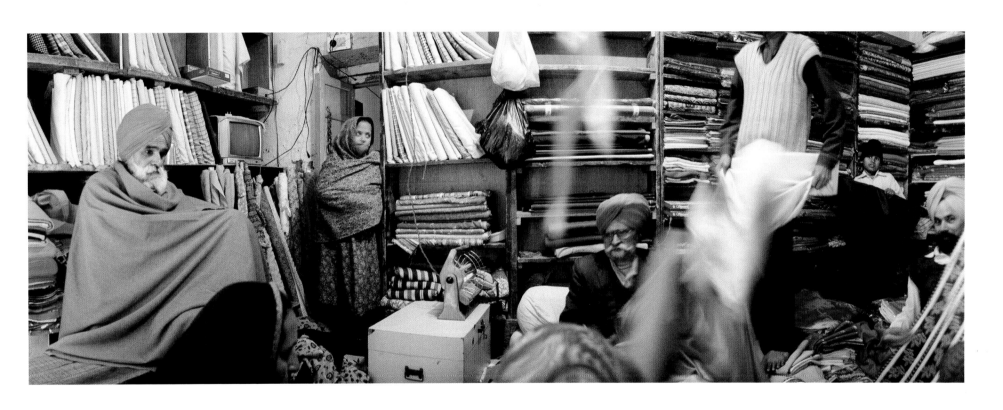

Amritsar, Selling Fabrics, 2003
Amritsar, Old Town Market, 2003 ▷

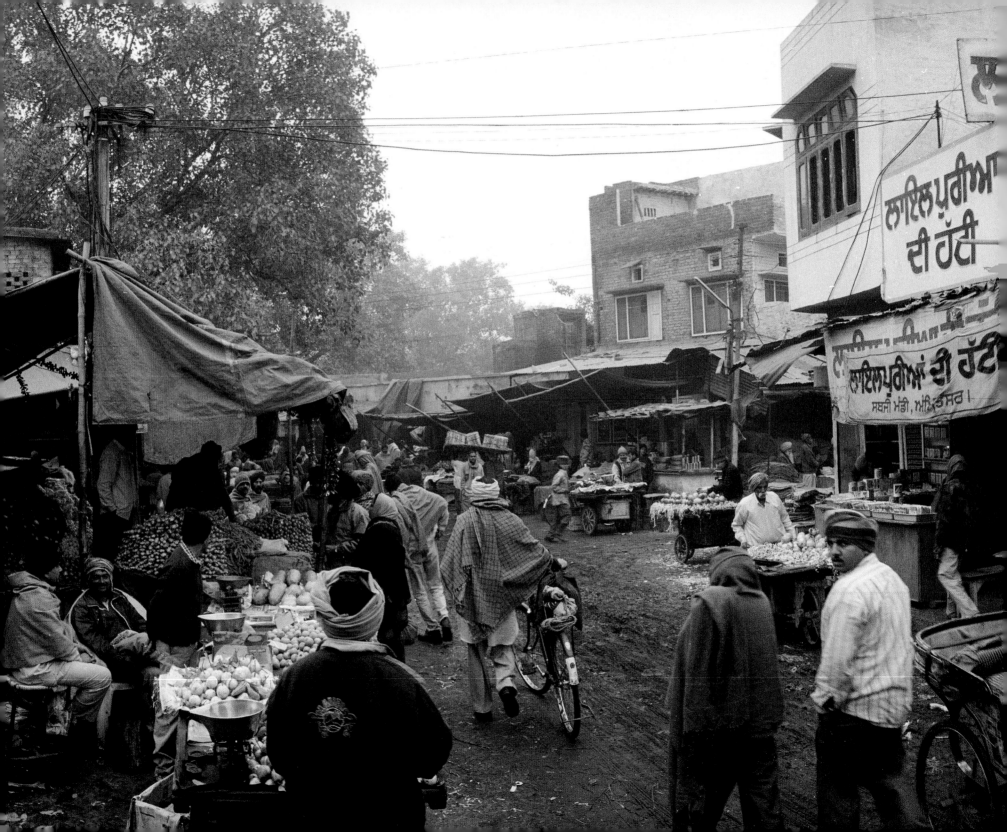

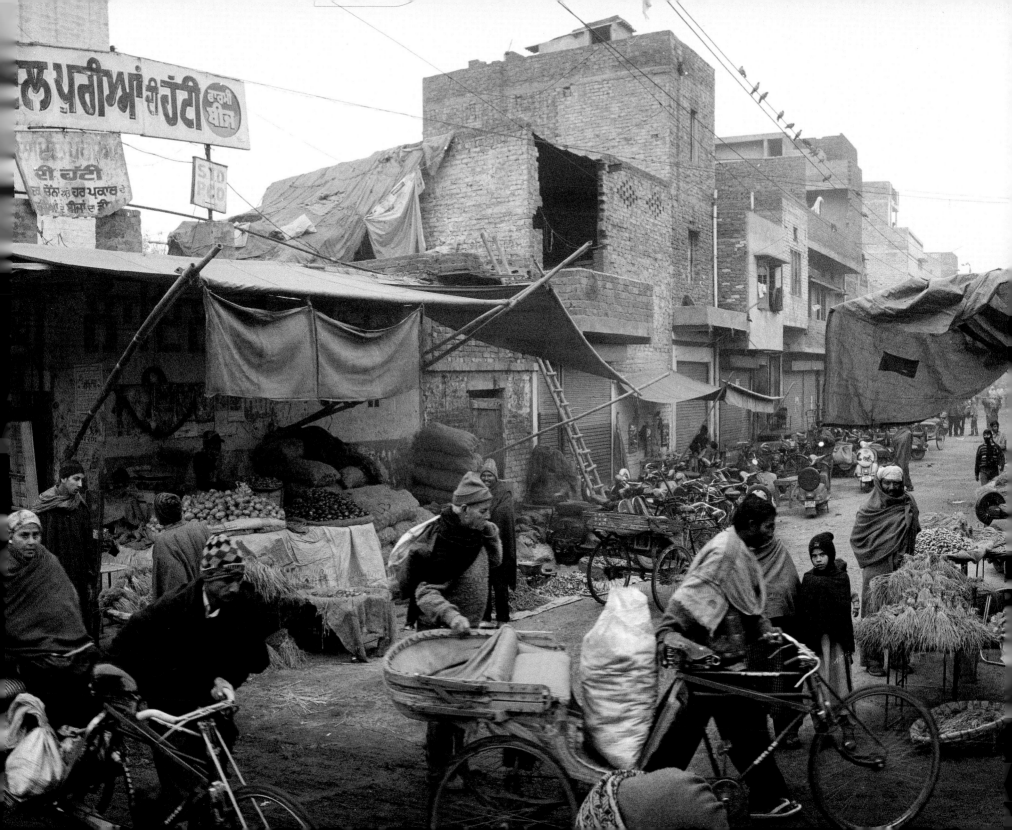

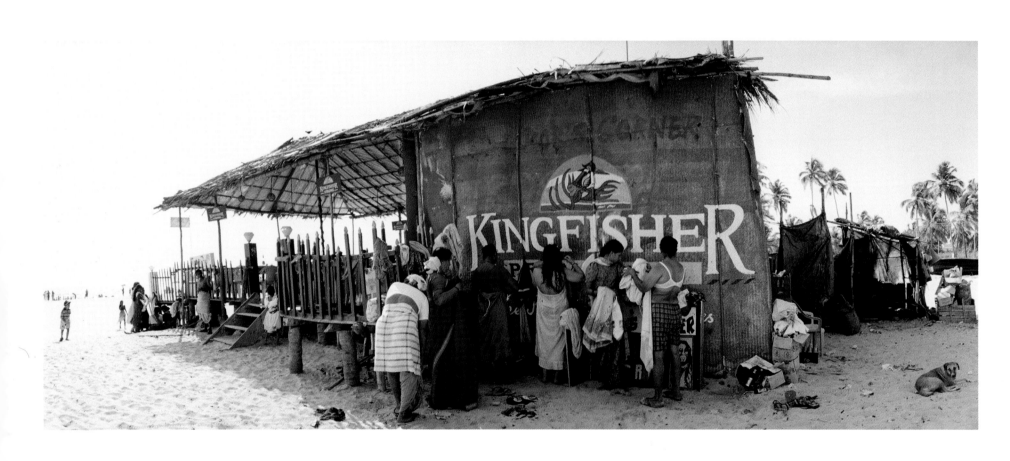

Goa-Calangute, Dressing Room, 2001

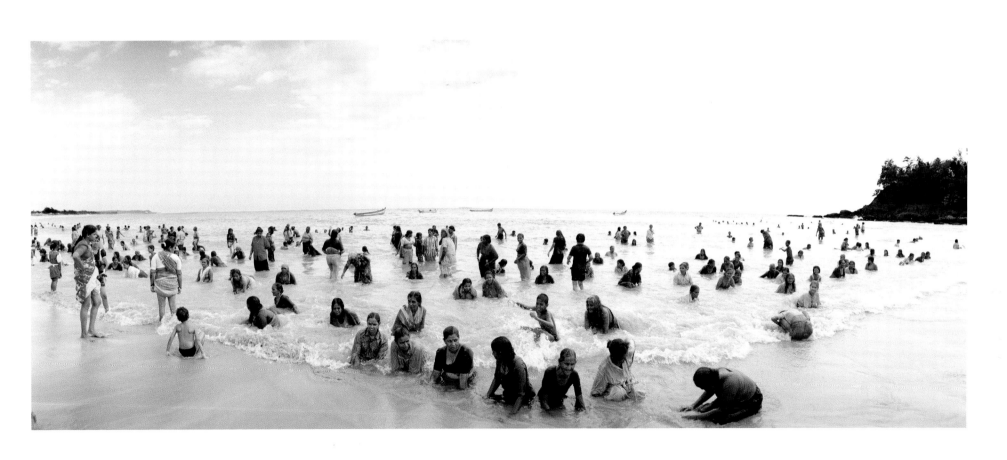

Goa, Late Afternoon Bath, 2001
Chennai, Sunset on the Beach, 1999 ▷

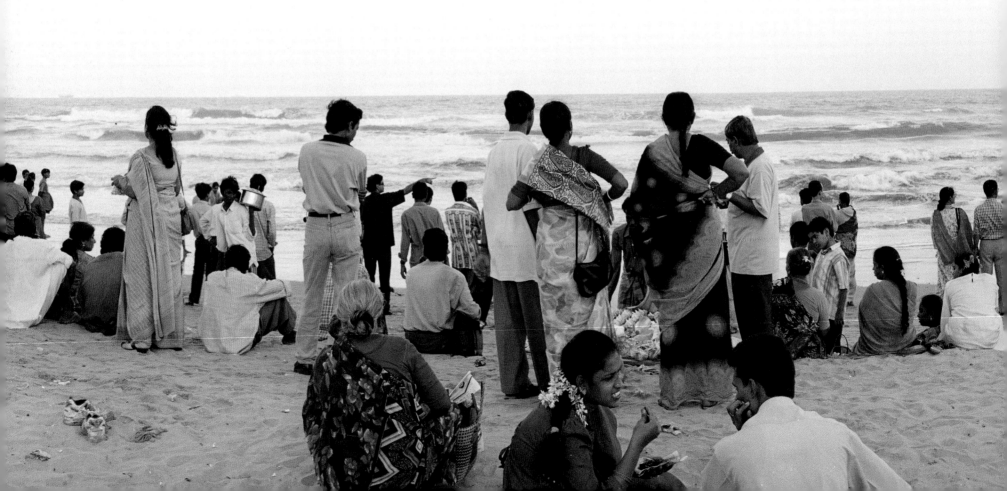

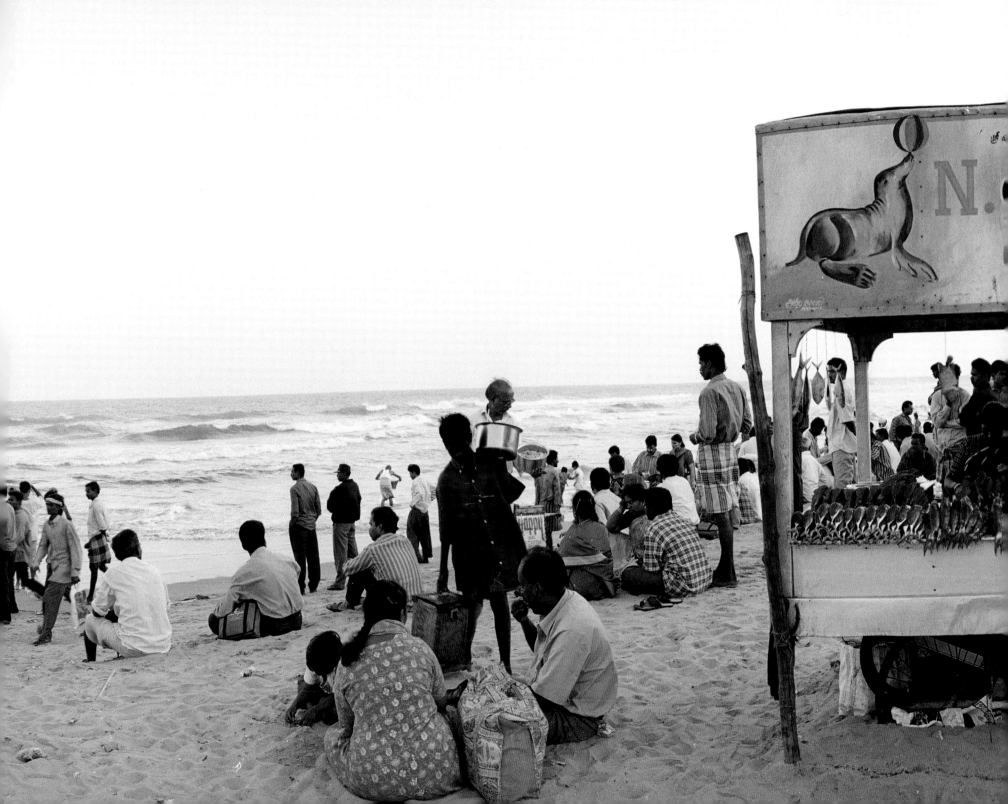

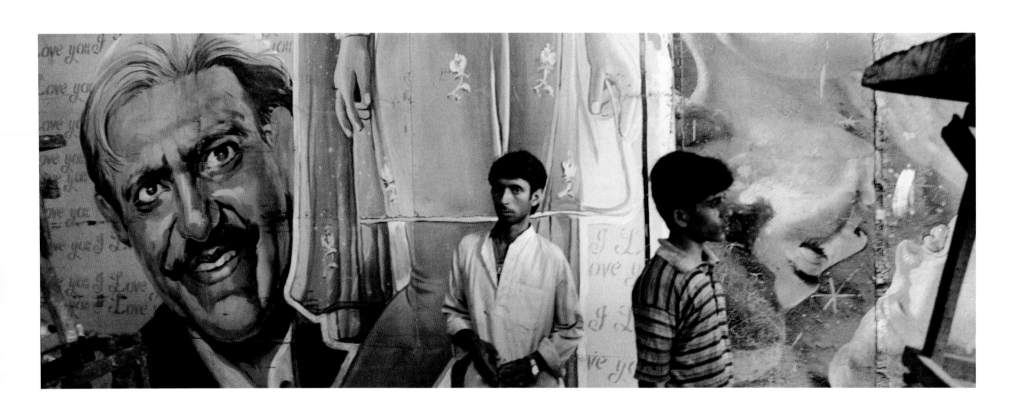

Chennai, Billboard Painters, 2001

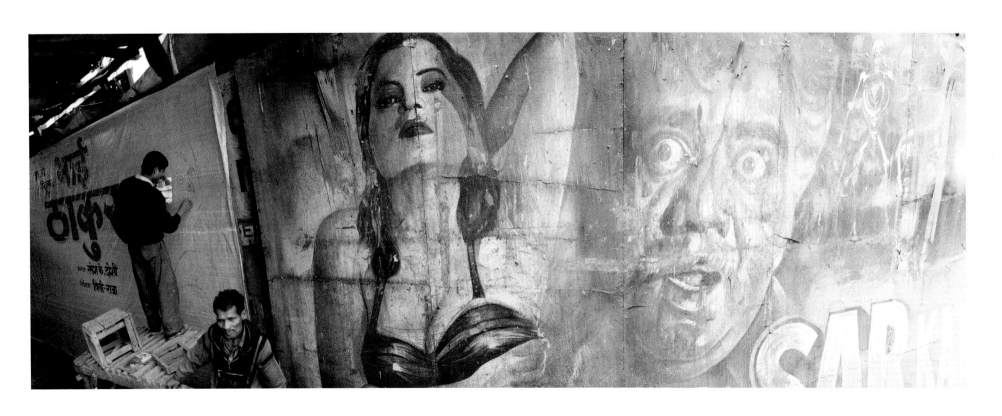

Delhi, Billboard Painters, 2001

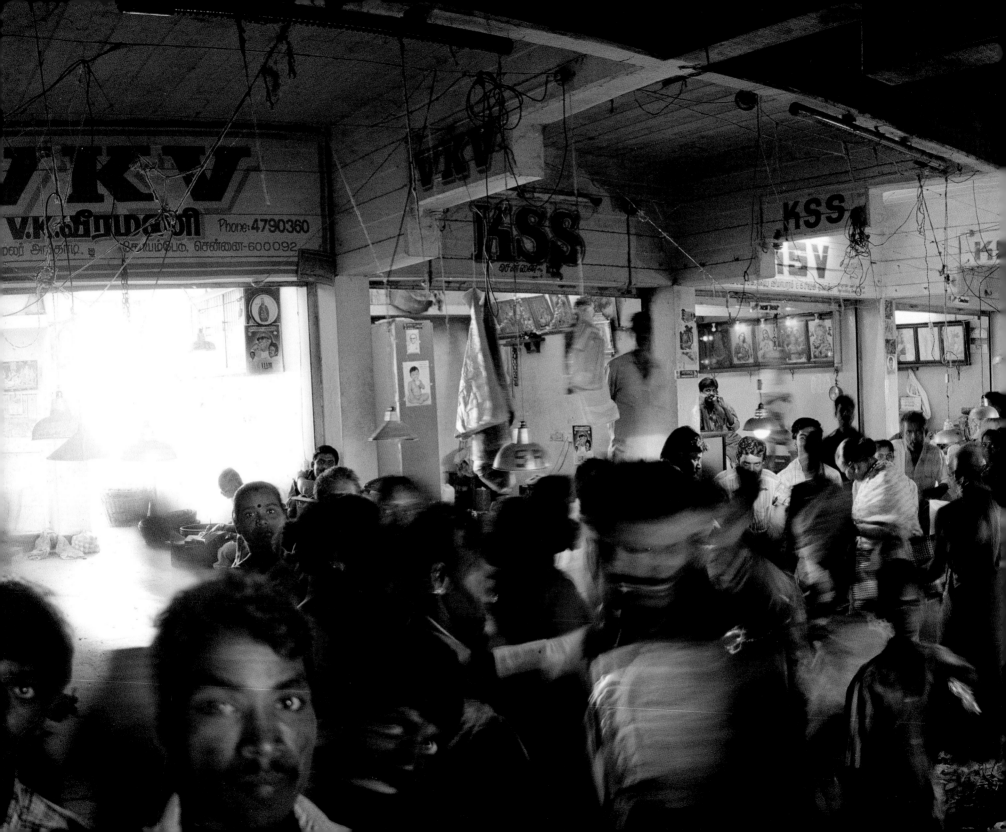

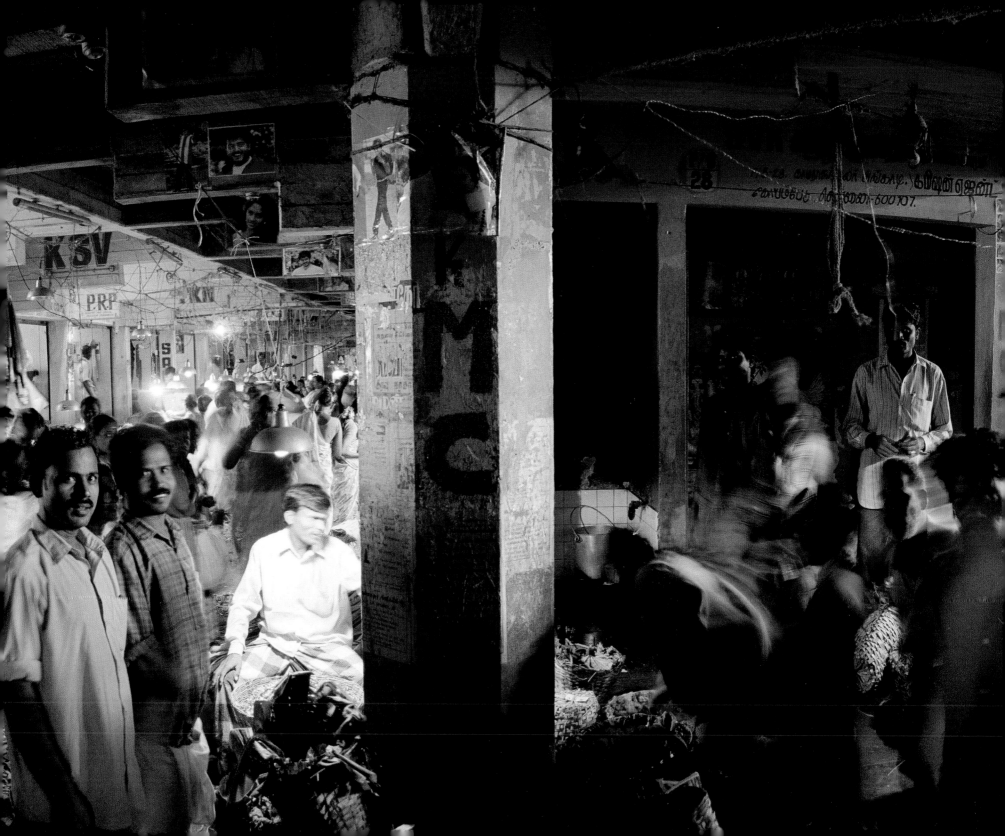

◁ Chennai, Covered Market, 1999

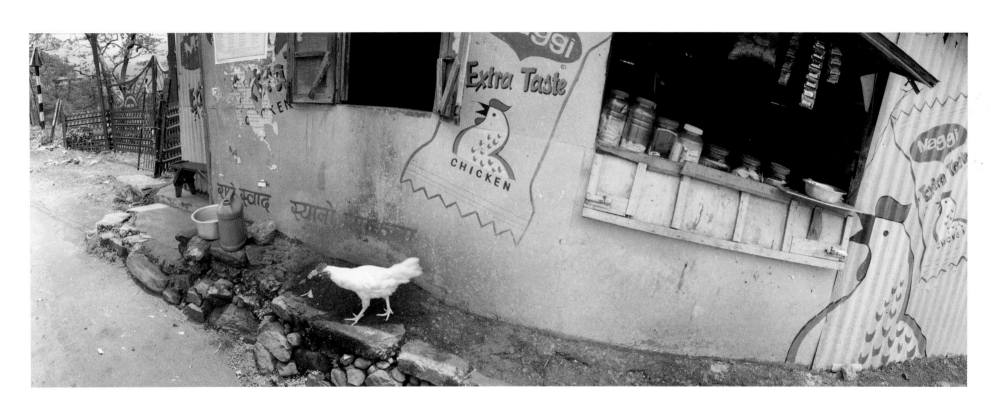

Darjeeling, Chicken Taste, 2002
Darjeeling, Near the Train Station, 2002 ▷

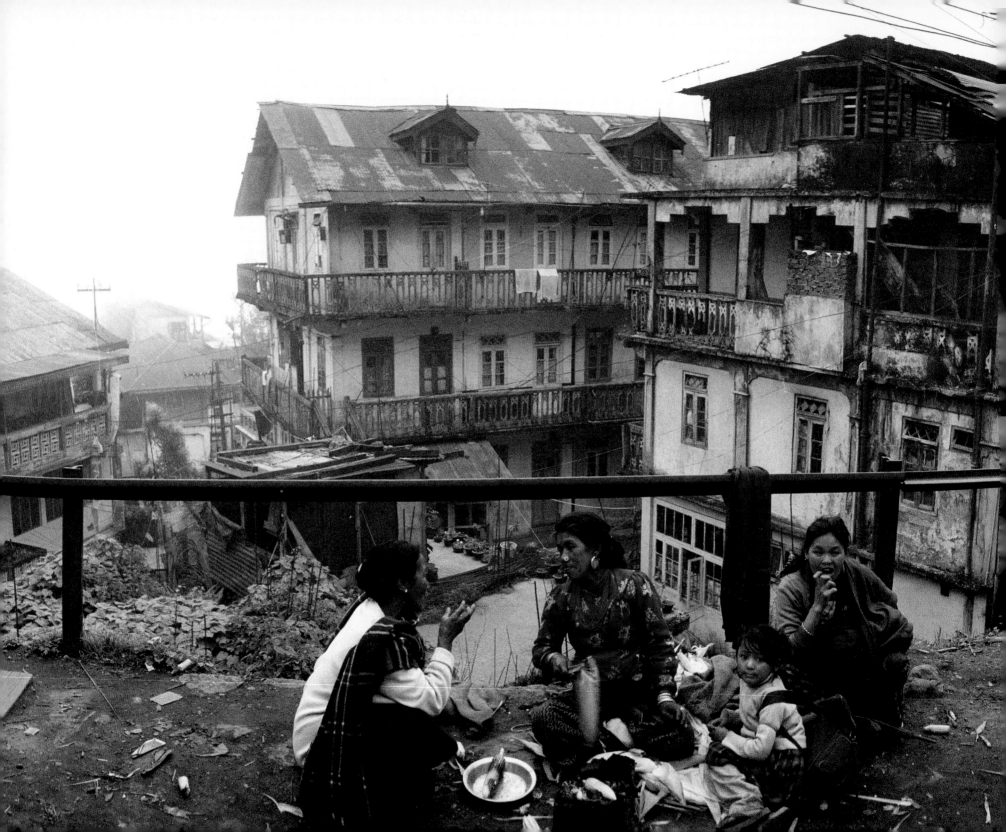

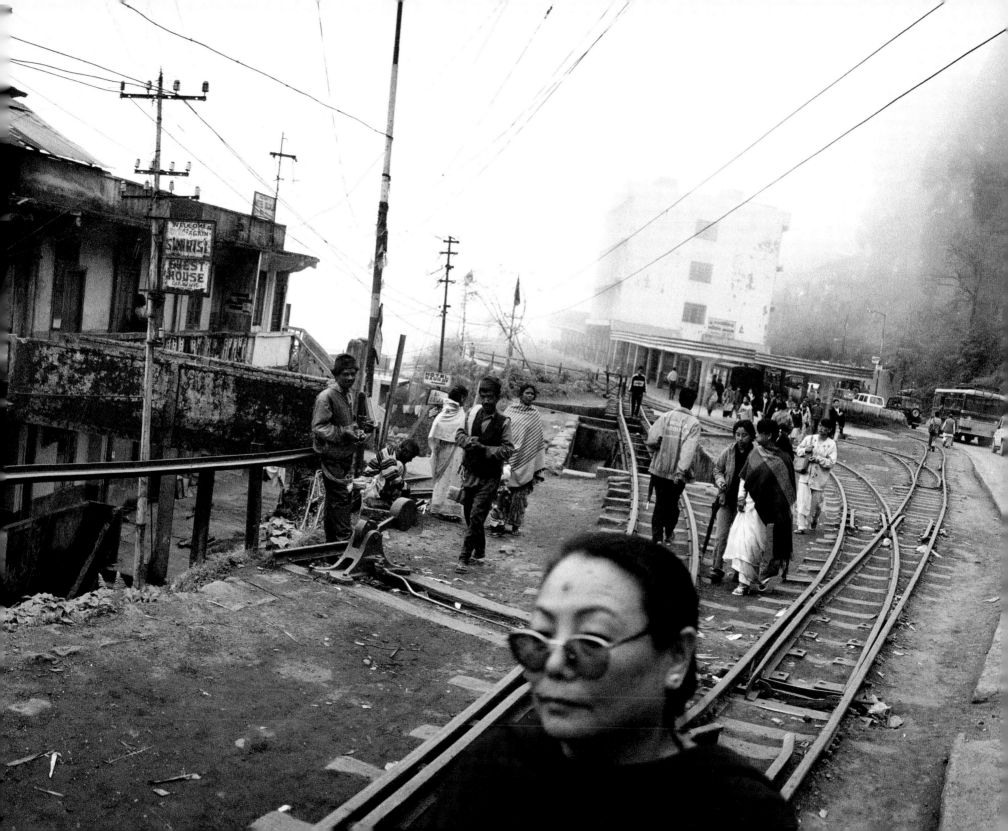

Delhi, Traffic Jam, 2001

*Taken in Delhi, this picture of two buses
(shot from the window of a taxi in the midst
of a traffic jam) summarizes, for me,
the difference between Old and New Delhi
—two very different towns.*

*Cette image de deux bus prise dans un taxi
pendant un embouteillage résume pour moi la
différence entre l'ancien et le nouveau Delhi.
Deux villes très différentes.*

*Questa foto di due autobus scattata da un taxi
durante un ingorgo stradale è per me la sintesi
della differenza fra la vecchia e la nuova Delhi:
due città molto diverse.*

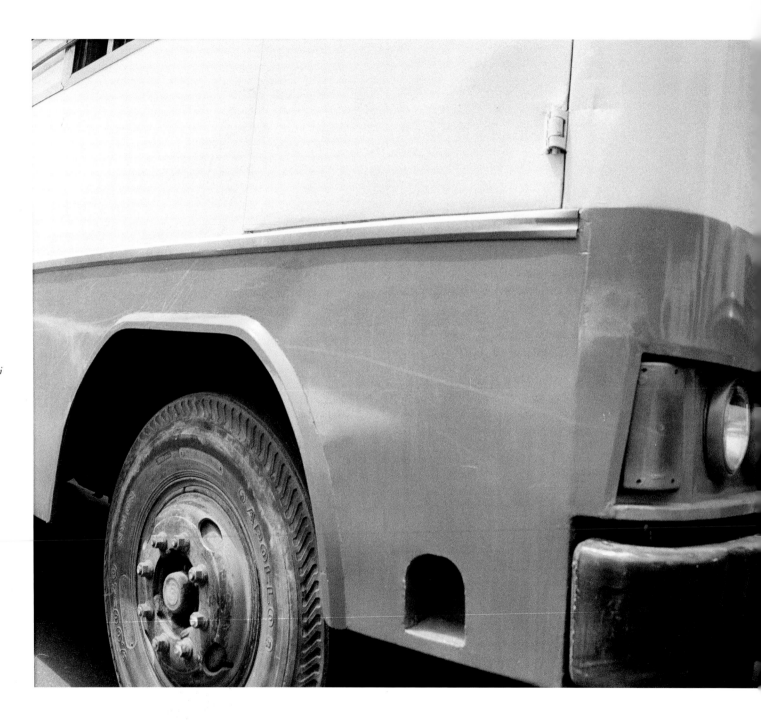

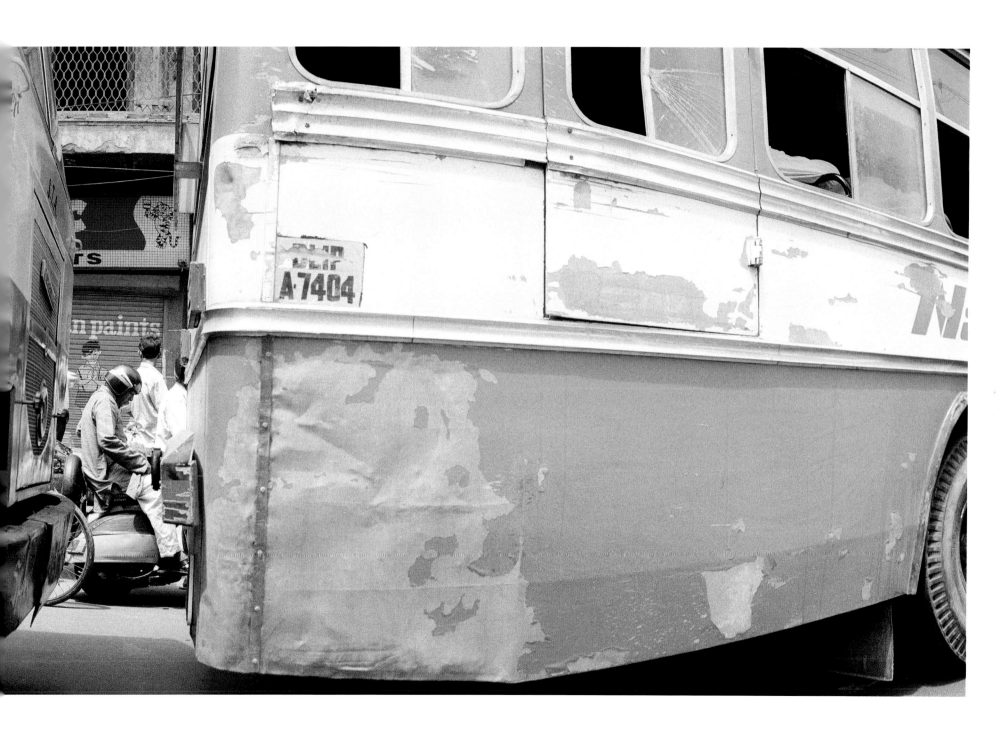

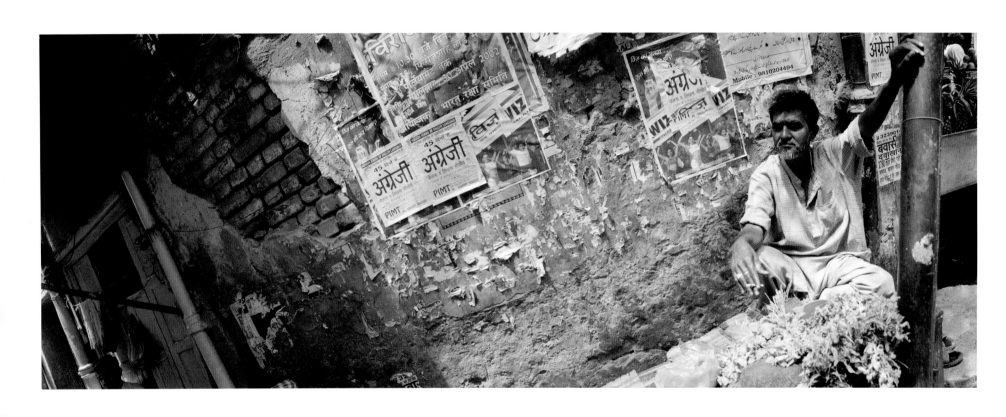

Delhi, Vegetable Salesman, 2002

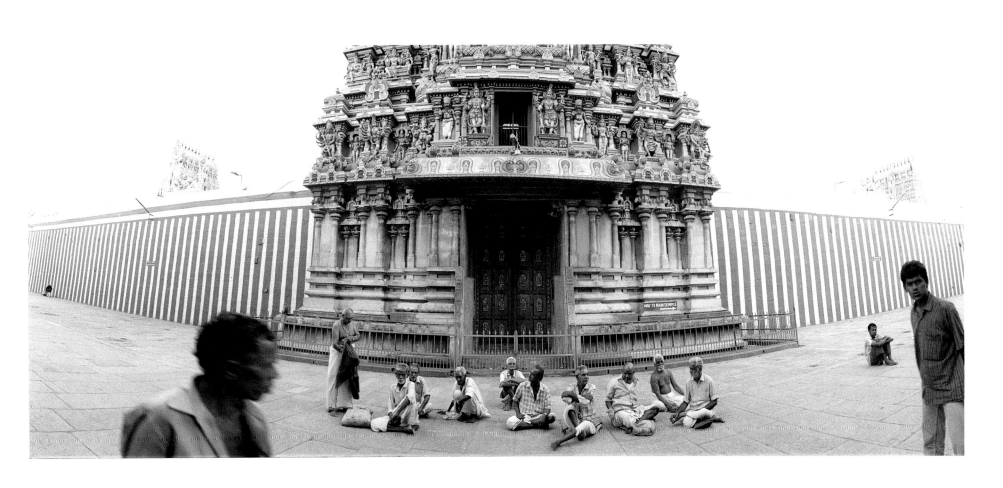

Kanchipuram, Various Poses, 2000
Rishikesh, Early Morning Tea, 2000 ▷

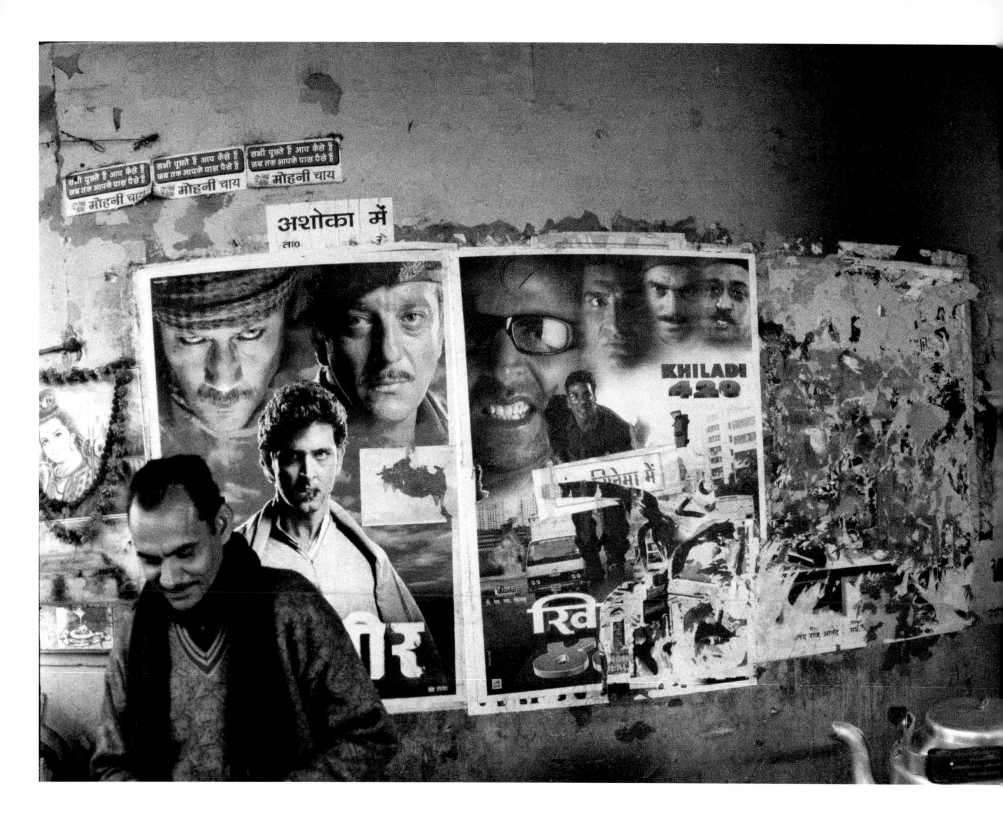

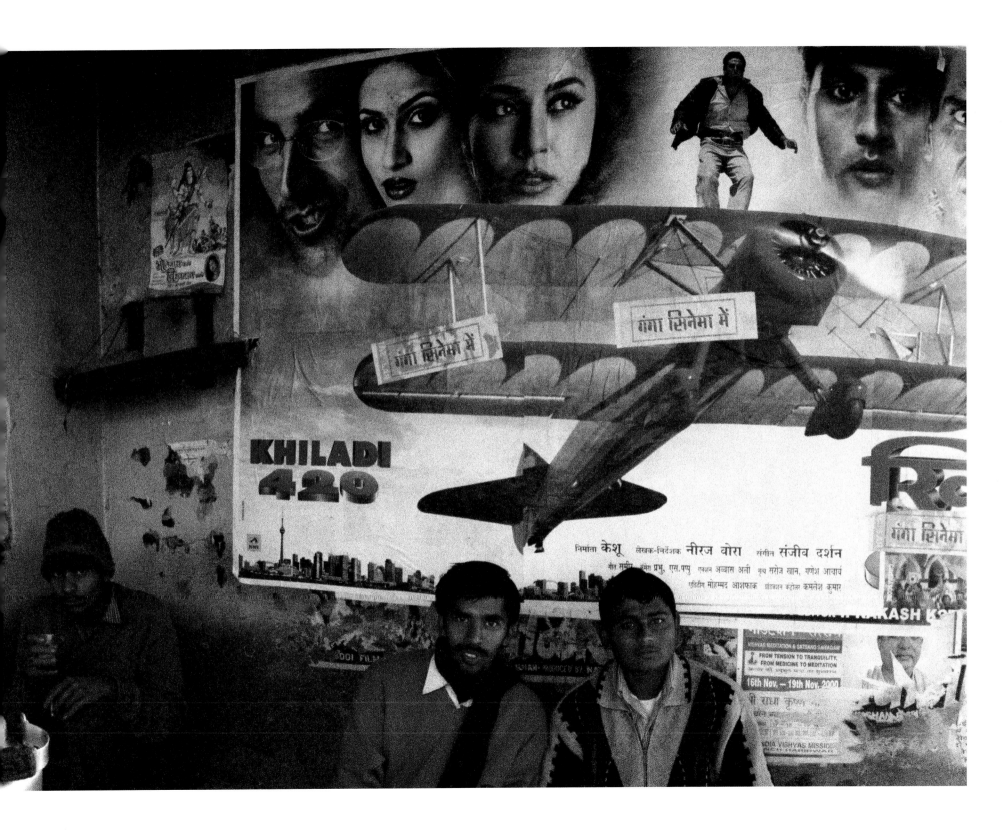

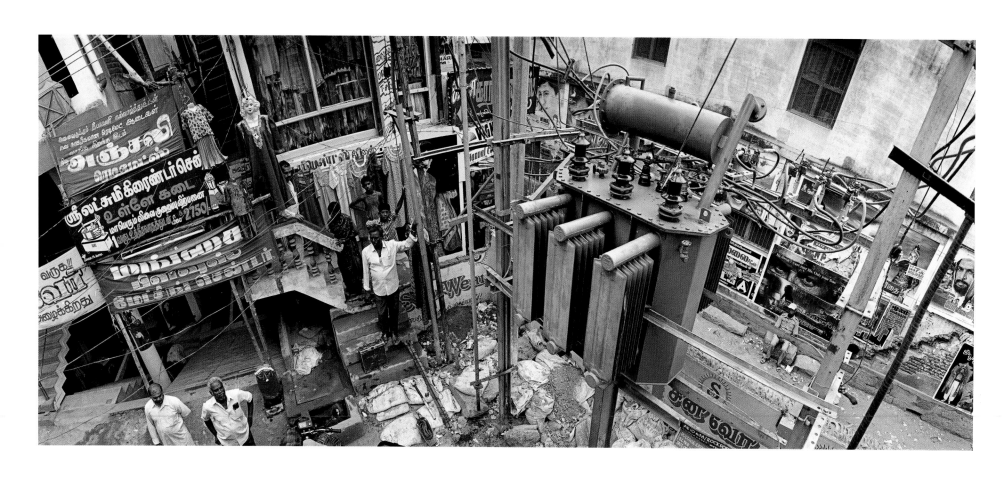

Salem, Transformer, 1999

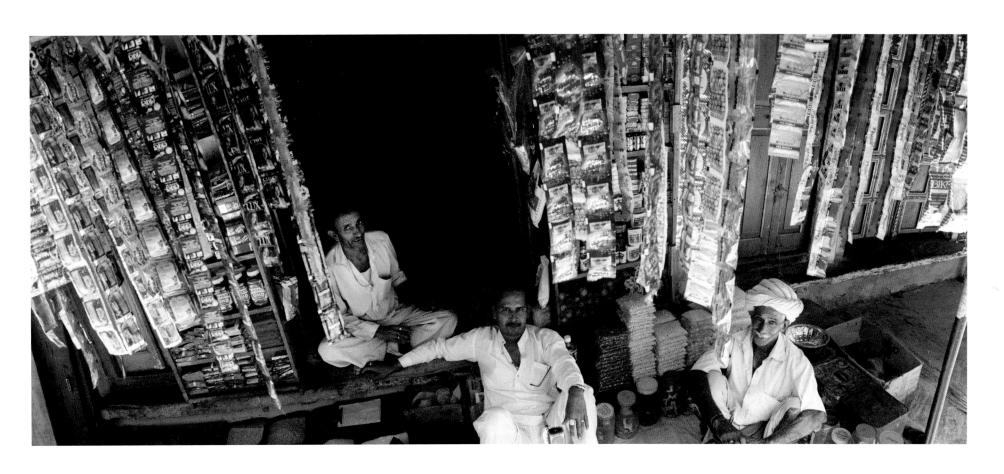

Rajasthan, Tobacco, 2002
Shillong, Vegetable Market, 2002 ▷

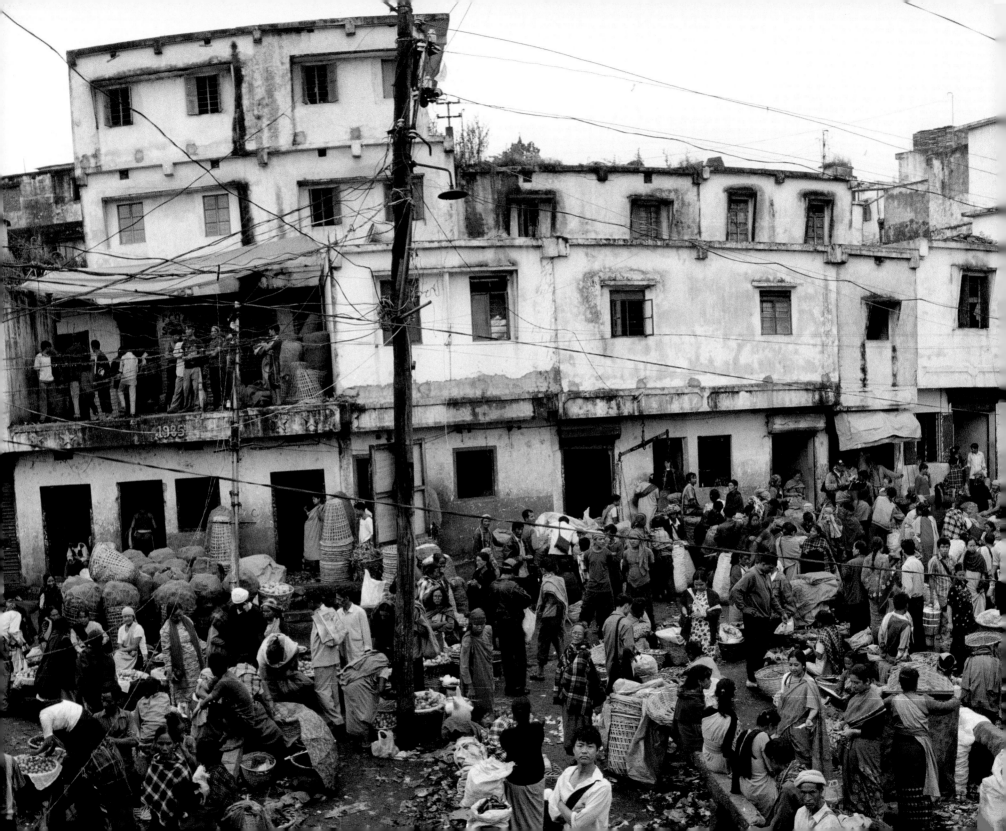

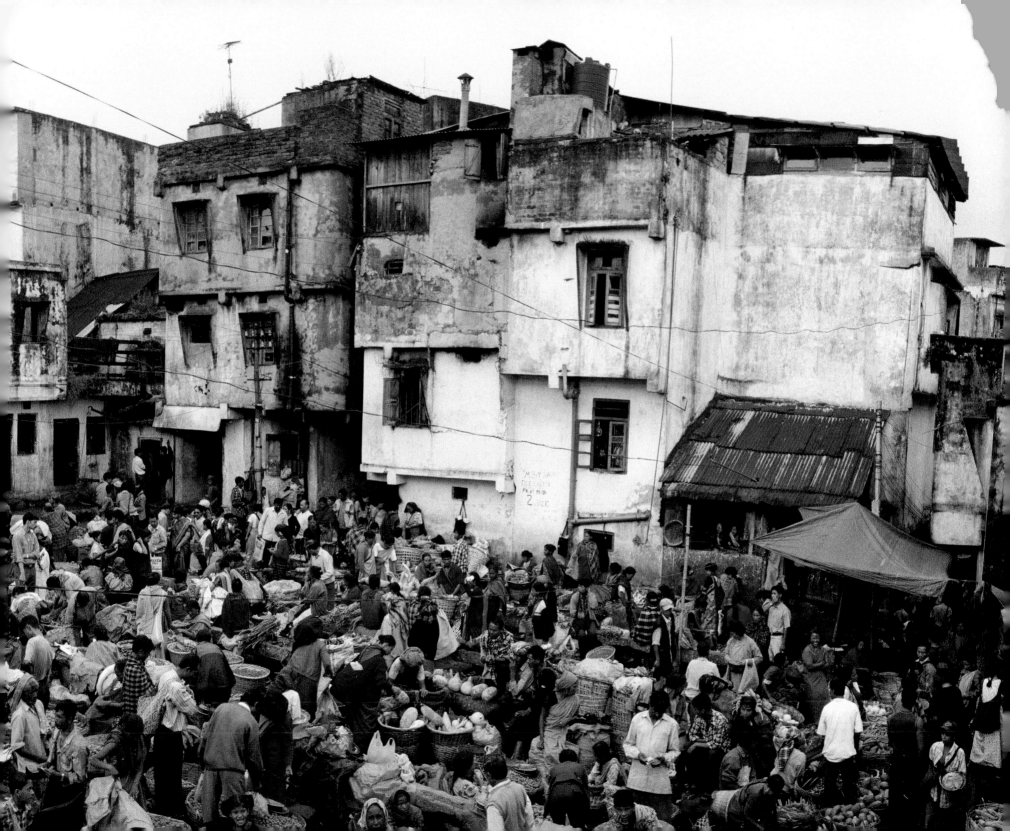

Jaisalmer, Wedding Snap, 2002

A young couple at a photo studio preparing
for wedding pictures. She is crisp and vivid.
He takes the situation very seriously.

Un jeune couple se prépare à ses photos
de mariage dans un studio de photographe.
Elle est vive et sûre. Il prend la situation
très au sérieux.

Una giovane coppia in uno studio fotografico
si prepara a farsi fotografare dopo le nozze.
Lei è vivace e sicura, lui prende la situazione
con molta serietà.

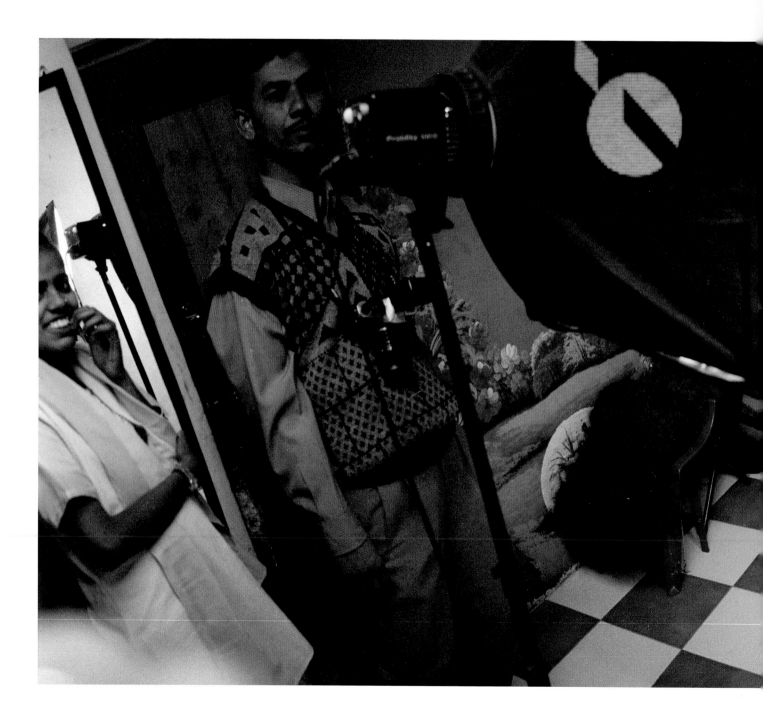

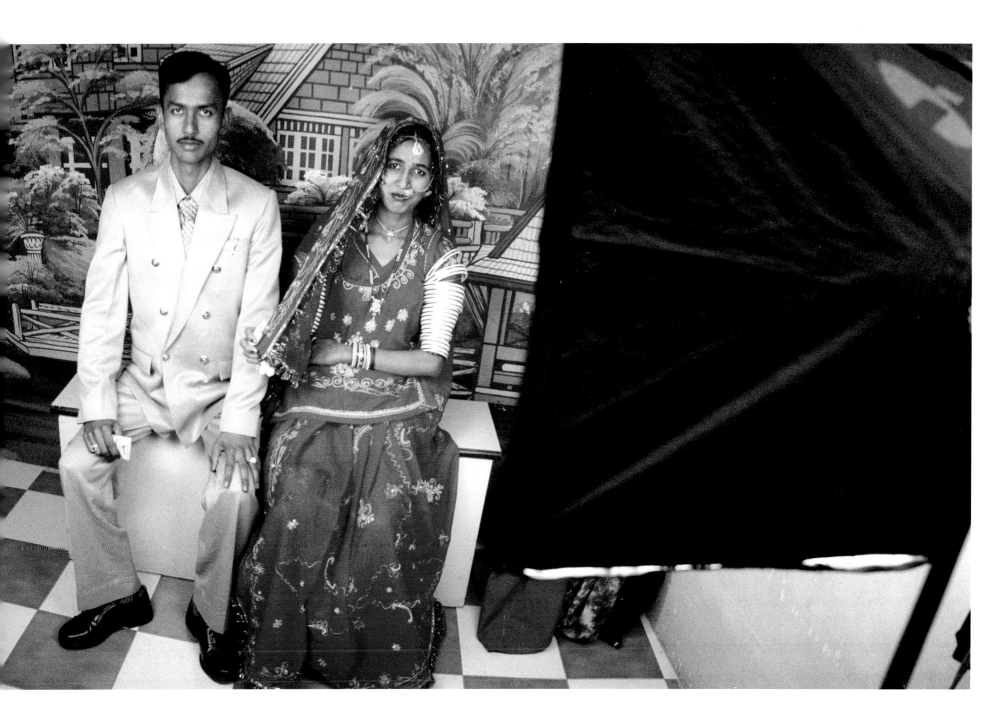

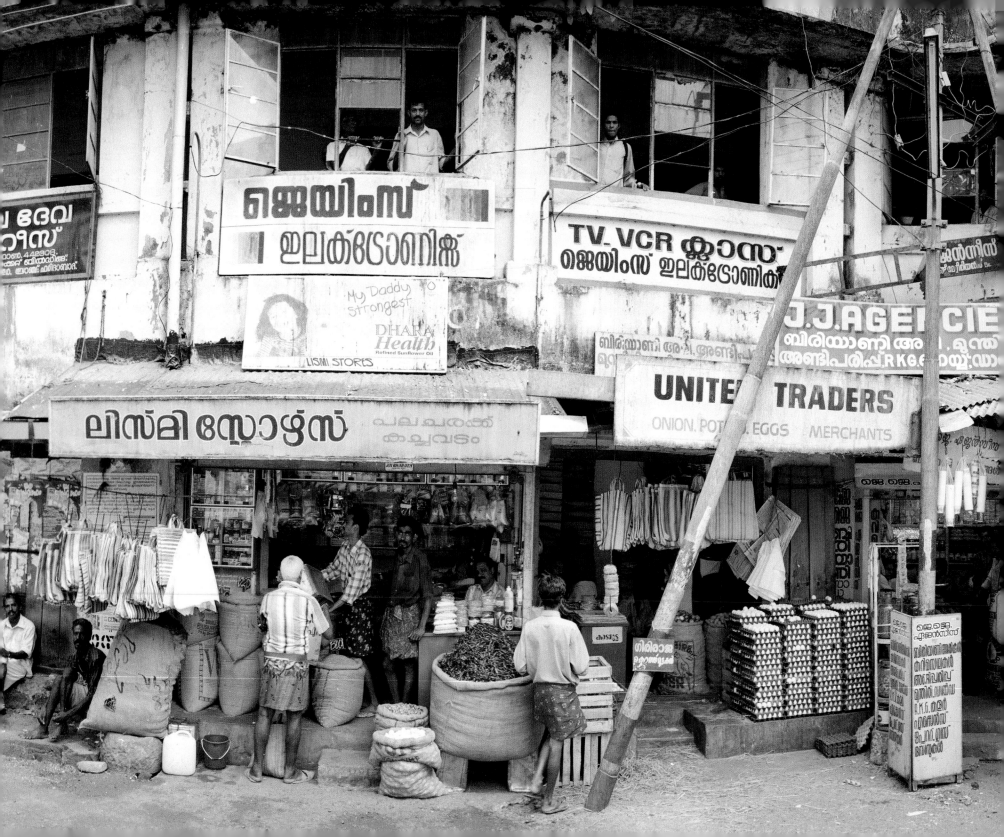

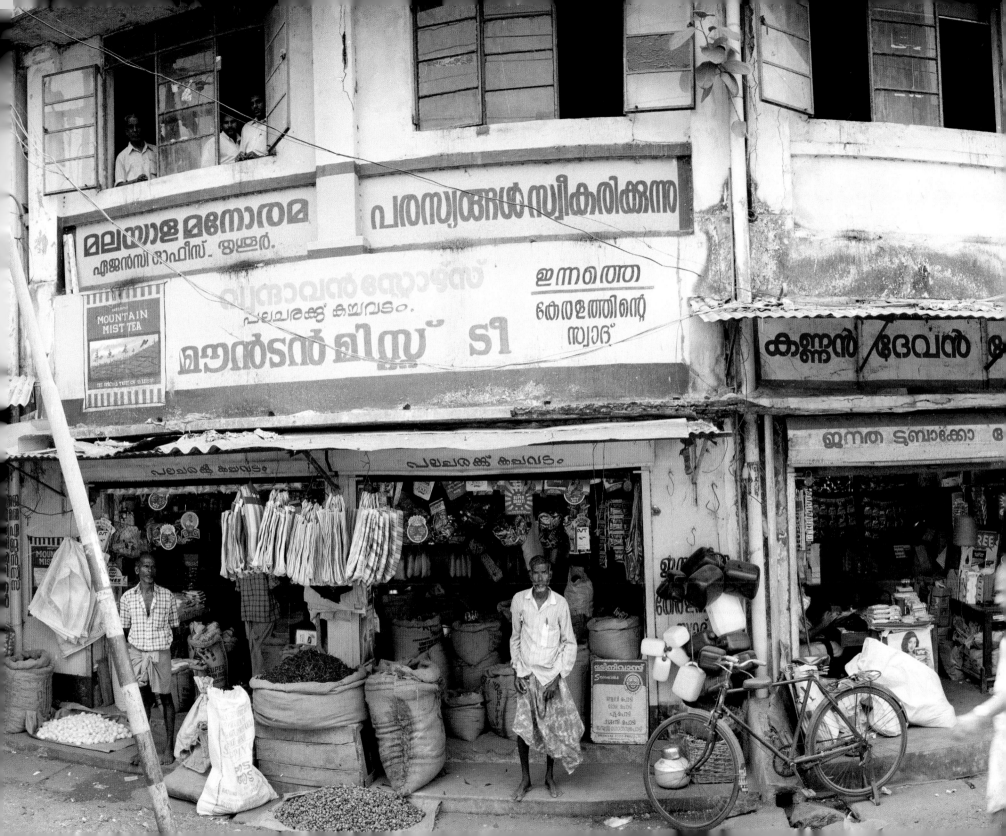

◁ Tamil Nadu, Merchants Street, 2001

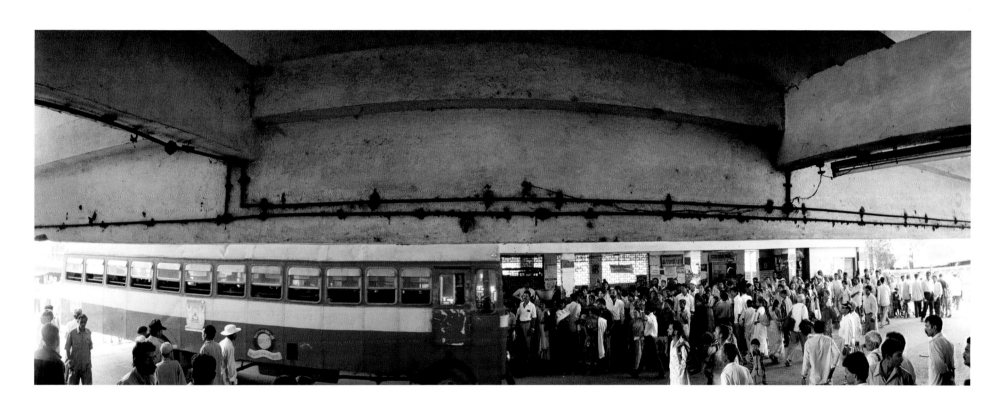

Tiruchirappalli, Bus Terminal, 2001

Udaipur, Dancers, 2002

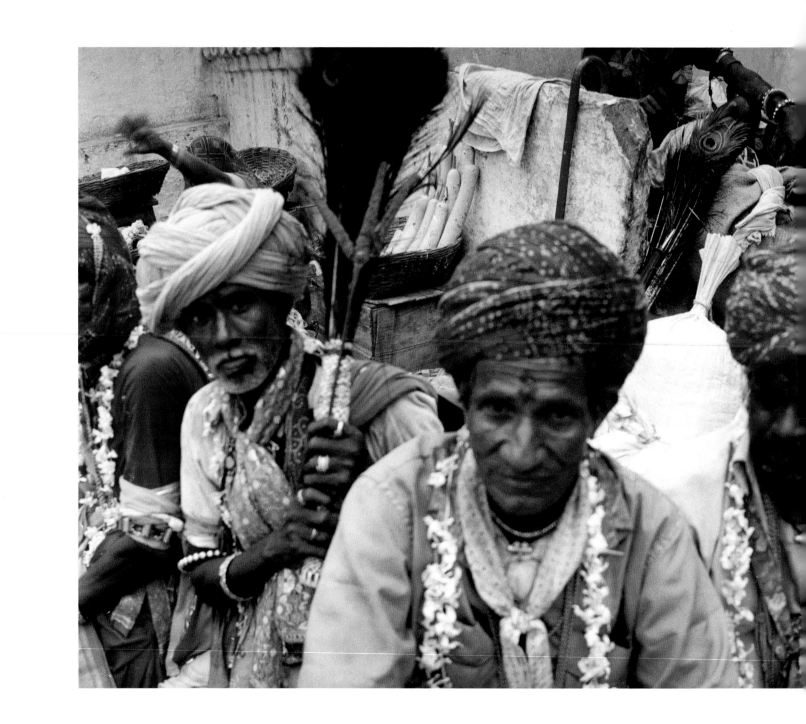

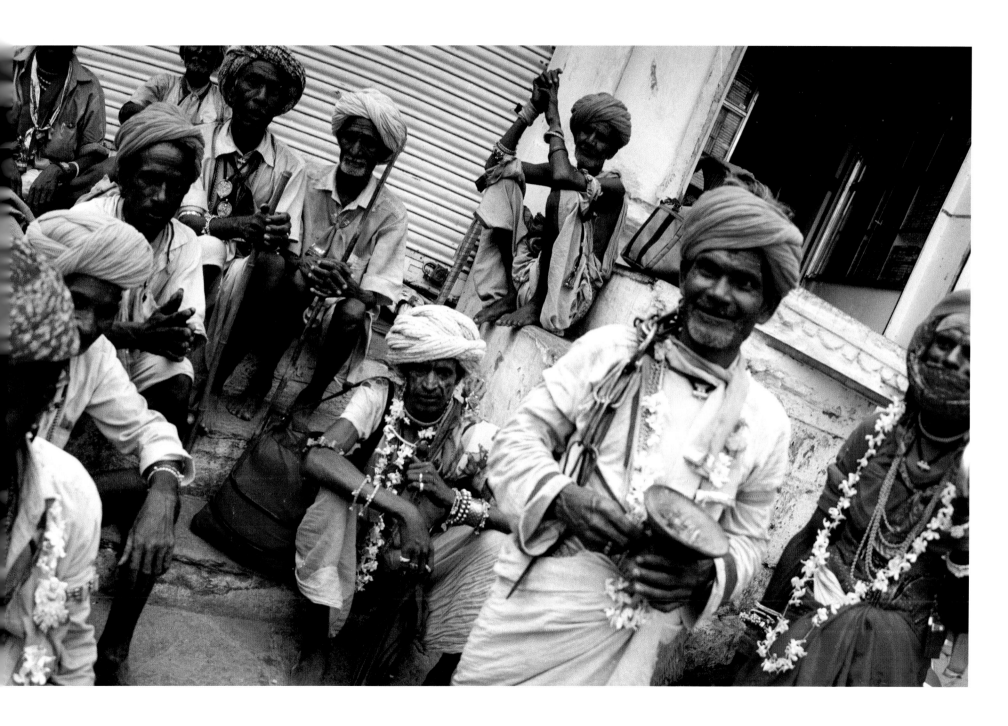

Udaipur, Trimming, 2002

In the former palace of a Maharaja, now
transformed into a five-star hotel, gardeners trim
trees near the pool, turning them into giant
umbrellas.

Dans l'ancien palais du maharaja, aujourd'hui
transformé en hôtel cinq étoiles, des jardiniers
taillent les arbres du bord de la piscine en forme
de parasols géants.

Nell'ex palazzo di un maharaja trasformato in un
albergo a cinque stelle, i giardinieri potano gli
alberi vicino alla piscina trasformandoli in
giganteschi ombrelloni.

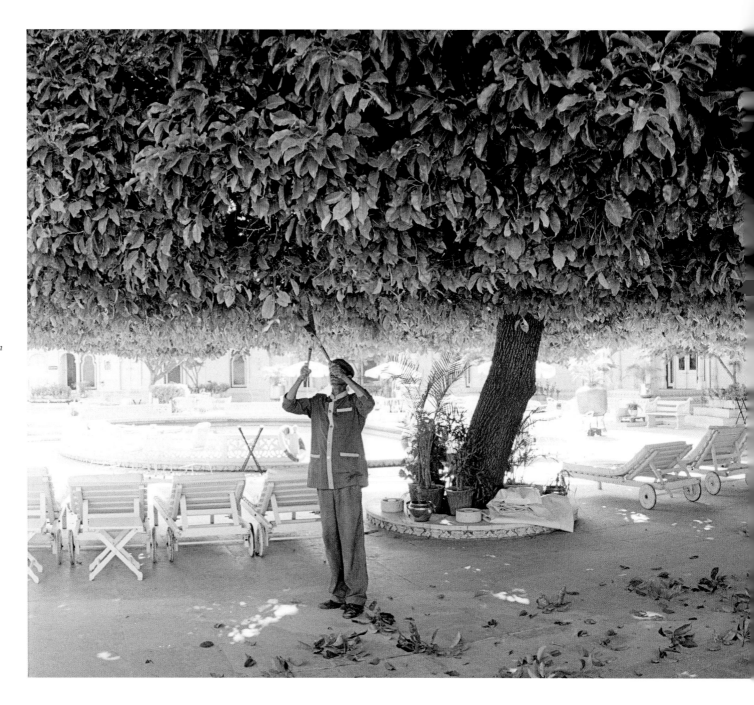

Uttar Pradesh, Transit Road, 2001 ▷▷

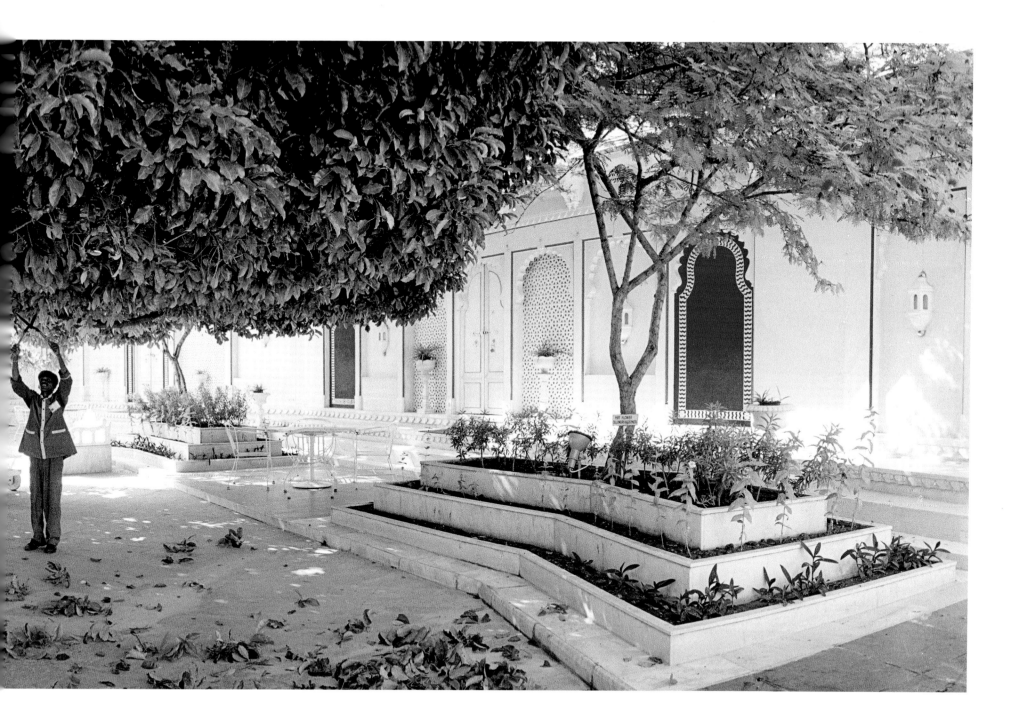

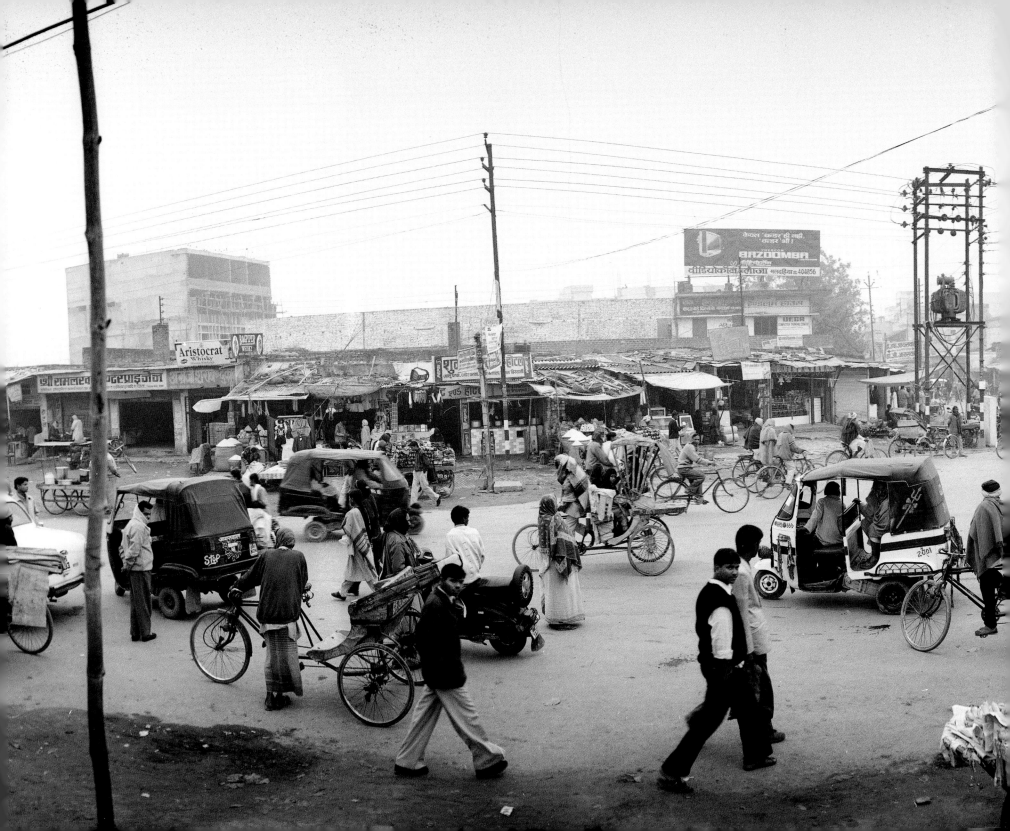

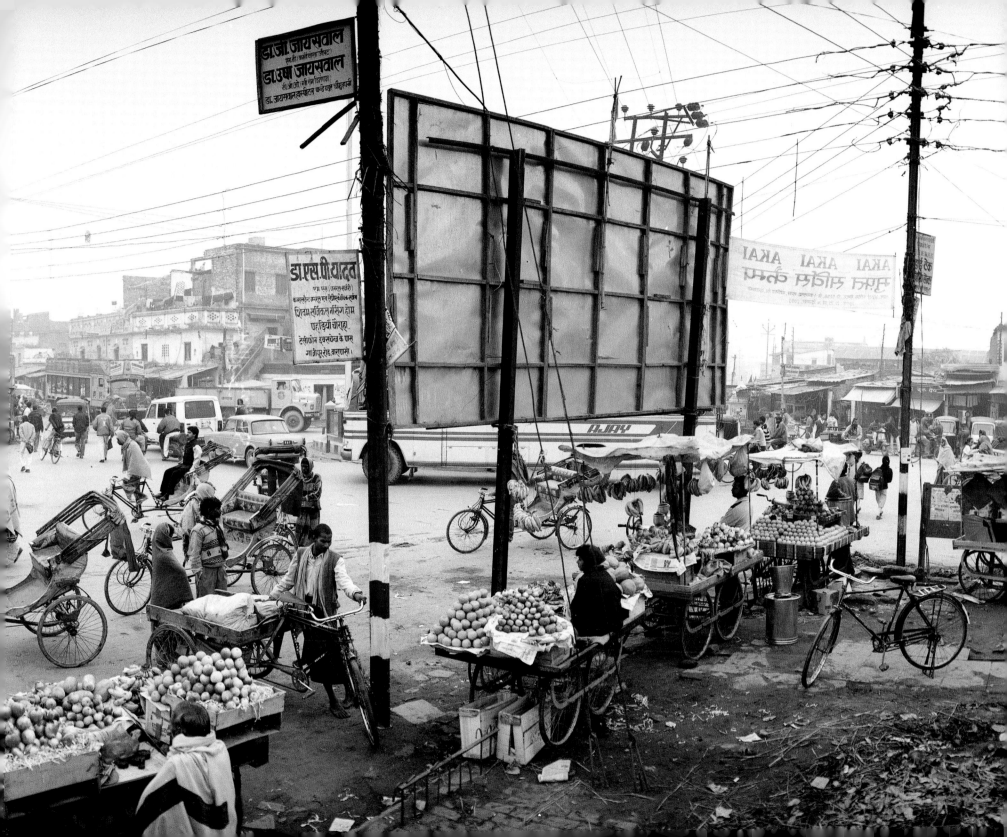

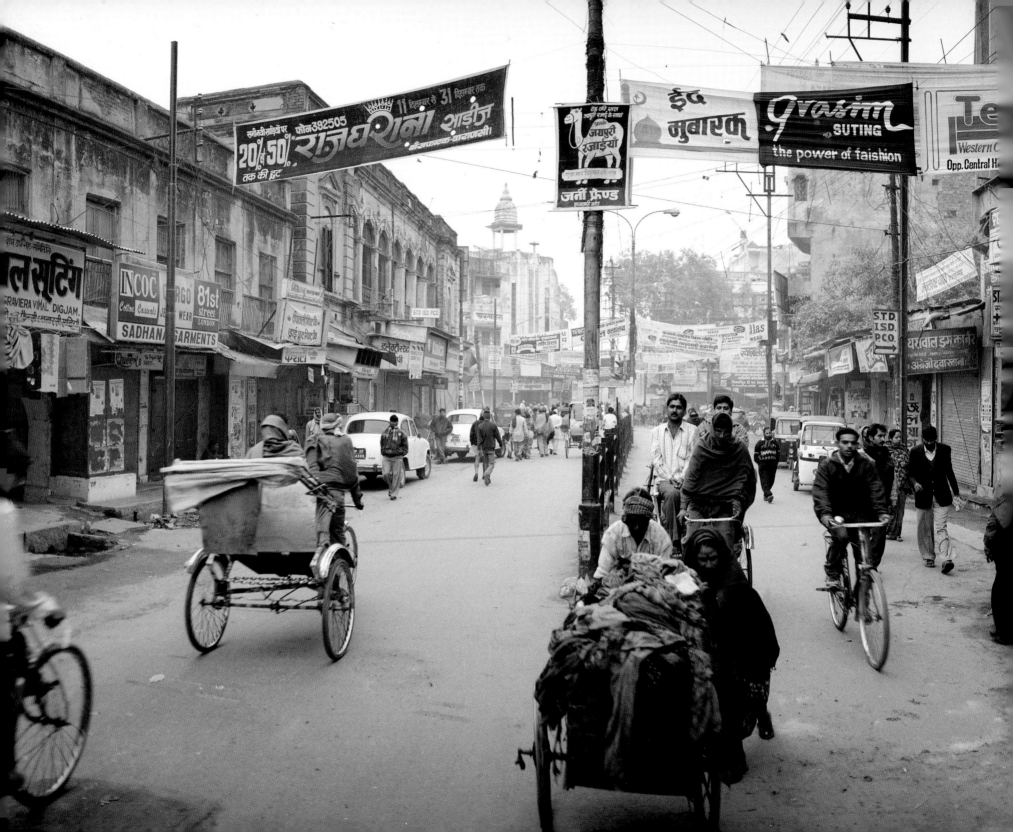

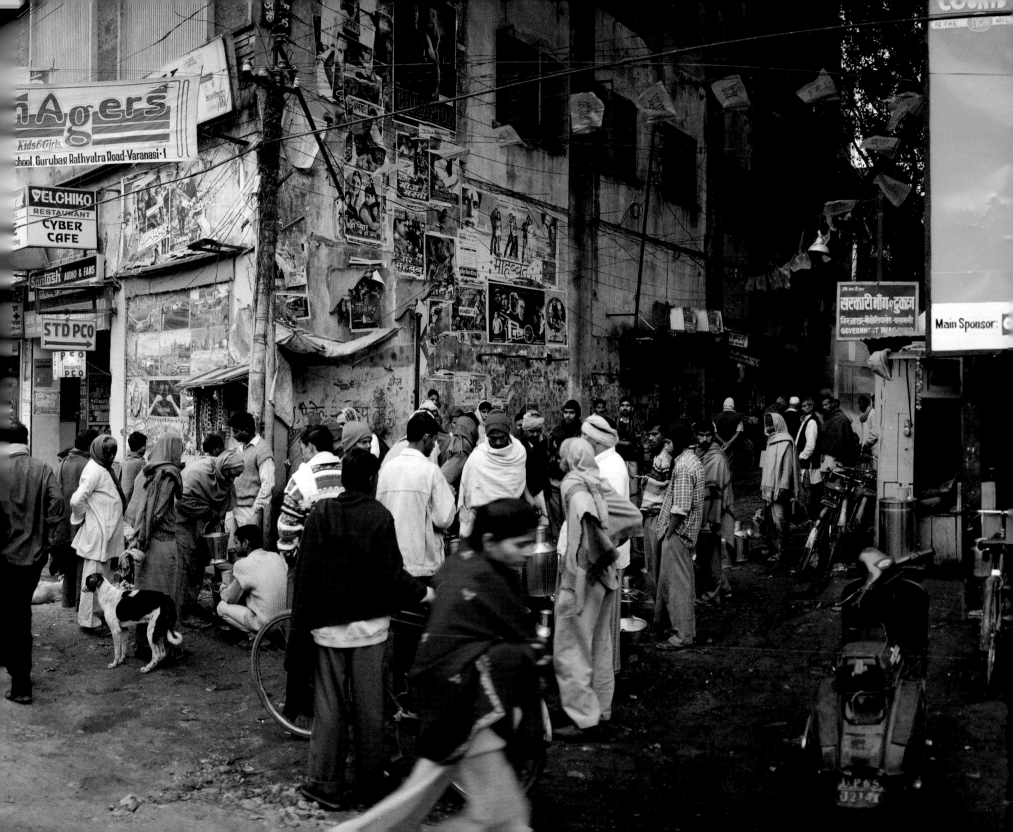

◁ Varanasi, Street Corner, 2001

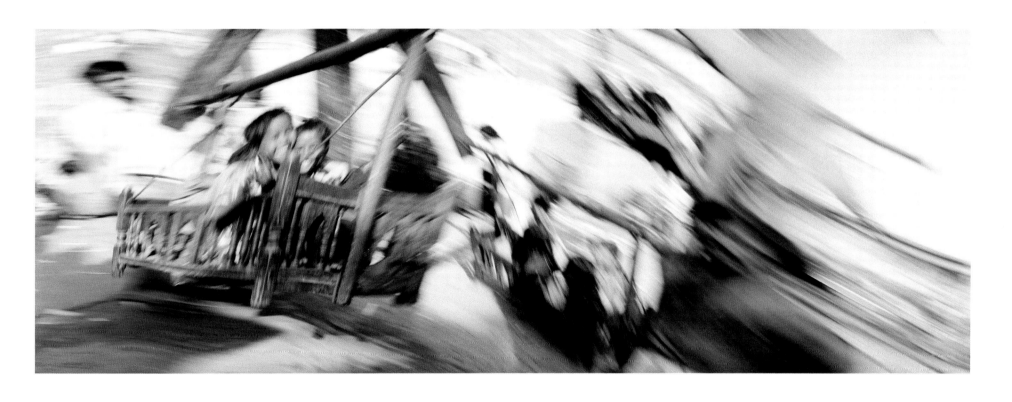

Desuri, Mela Attraction, 2002
Kochi, Workers at Rest, 2001 ▷

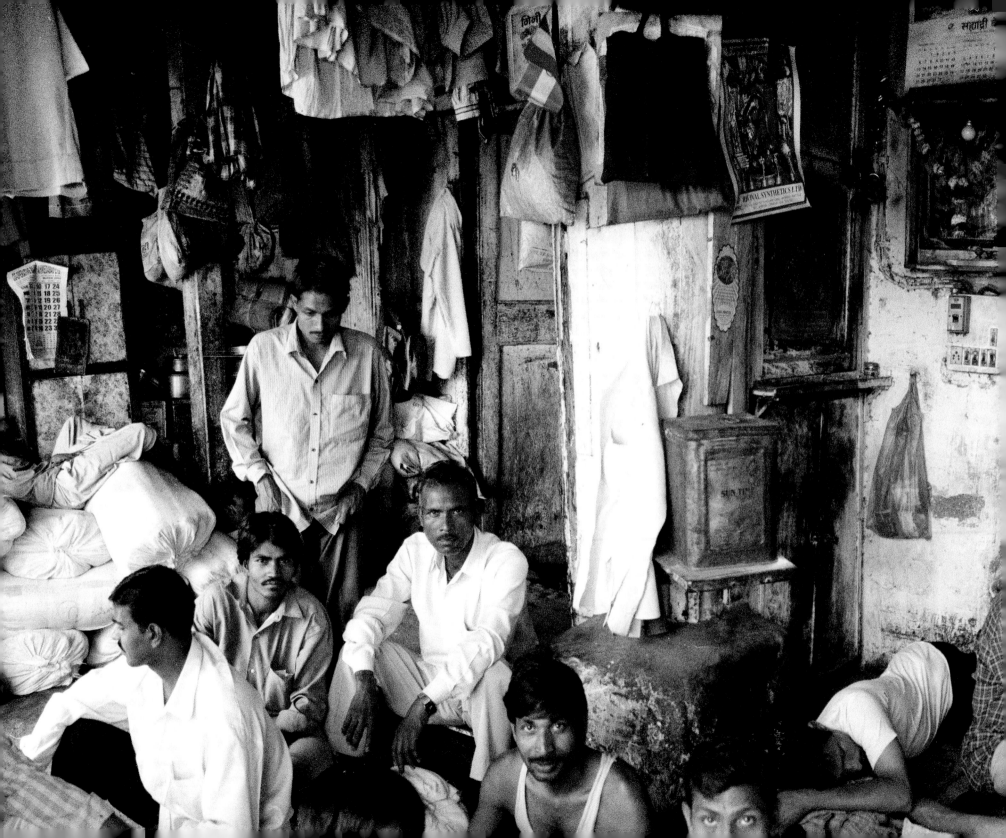

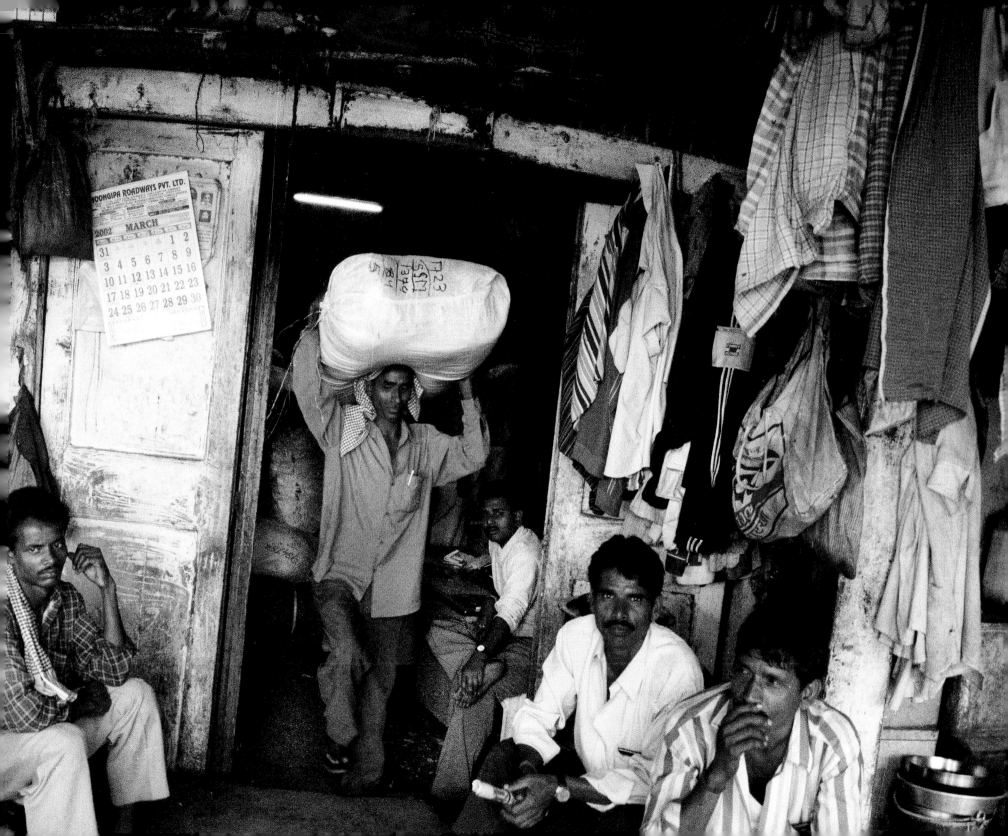

Punjab, Border Match, 2003

*Just as in a soccer stadium, every night
at the Pakistan border supporters of each country
come to watch the lowering of the flags. Game
or real hatred; war simulation or ritual sport?
The feelings are mixed.*

*Chaque nuit à la frontière pakistanaise,
comme dans un stade de football, les supporters
de chaque pays viennent assister au baisser
des couleurs. Jeu ou haine réelle, simulation
de guerre ou rituel sportif? Les sentiments
sont mélangés.*

*Ogni sera, al confine col Pakistan,
i sostenitori dei due paesi vengono ad osservare
l'ammainabandiera come fossero allo stadio.
Gioco o vero odio, simulazione di guerra o sport
rituale? I sentimenti si mescolano.*

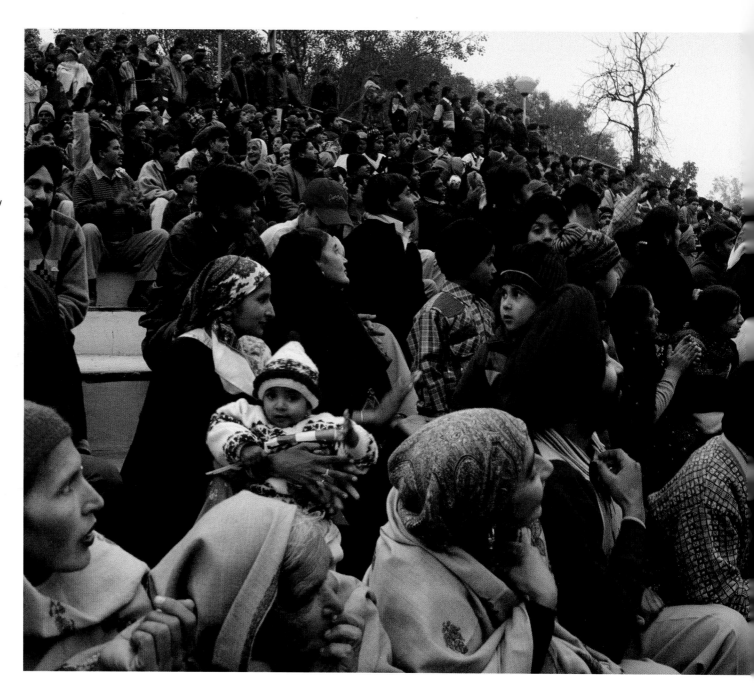

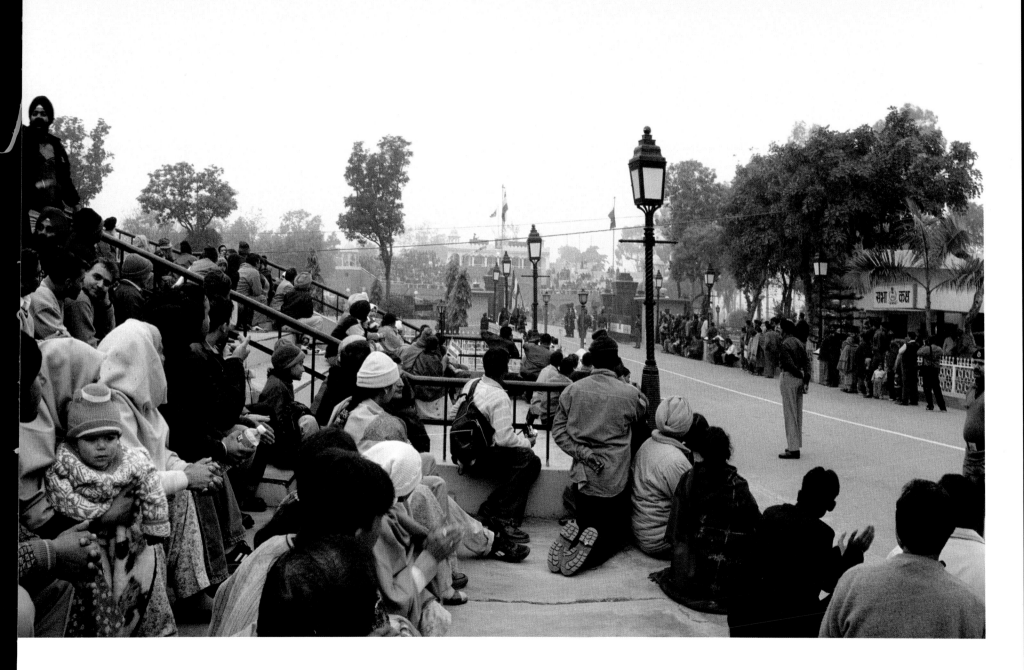